AGAINST TALL ODDS

AGAINST TALL ODDS

BEING A DAVID IN A GOLIATH WORLD

MATT ROLOFF

WITH TRACY SUMNER

Multnomah®Publishers *Sisters, Oregon*

AGAINST TALL ODDS
published by Multnomah Publishers, Inc.

© 1999 by Matt Roloff
International Standard Book Number: 1-57673-583-4

Design by Stephen Gardner
Cover photo by Paul Sanders

Scripture quoted unless otherwise noted:
The Holy Bible, New International Version (NIV) © 1973, 1984 by International Bible Society,
used by permission of Zondervan Publishing House

Also quoted:
Holy Bible, New Living Translation (NLT) © 1996.
Used by permission of Tyndale House Publishers, Inc. All rights reserved.
The Holy Bible, New Century Version (NCV) © 1987, 1988, 1991
by Word Publishing. Used by permission.

Multnomah is a trademark of Multnomah Publishers, Inc., and is registered
in the U.S. Patent and Trademark Office.
The colophon is a trademark of Multnomah publishers, Inc.
Printed in the United States of America

For information:
Multnomah Publishers, Inc., Post Office Box 1720, Sisters, Oregon 97759

Library of Congress Cataloging–in–Publication Data
Roloff, Matt.
  Against tall odds: being a David in a Goliath world/by Matt Roloff, with Tracy Sumner.
  p.cm.   ISBN 1-57673-583-4 (alk. paper)   1. Roloff, Matt. 2. Dwarfs–United States
Biography. 3. Diastrophic dwarfism. I. Sumner, Tracy. II. Title.
CT9992.R64A3   1999   99-32270
362.1'9647–dc21   [B]   CIP

99 00 01 02 03 04 05 — 10 9 8 7 6 5 4 3 2 1

DEDICATION

To Ron and Peggy Roloff, my parents,
for their love, compassion, toughness, and wisdom
in raising me to have an overcoming attitude.

TABLE OF CONTENTS

ACKNOWLEDGMENTS

An amazing thing happened to me on the way to completing this project: I realized how many people I am grateful to for the positive influences they've had in my life, for helping instill in me an overcoming attitude. I have many family, friends, and other associates I'd like to thank, not just for making this book possible, but for helping to make my life what it has become.

Thanks to my family—my wife and kids, as well as my mother, father, brothers, and sister—for helping to make my life the joy it has been.

My lovely and amazing wife, Amy, and my beautiful children, Jeremy, Zachary, Molly, and Jacob—you are truly God's greatest earthly blessing for me. You not only bring me joy and happiness, you are an instrument used daily by God to make me a better person. I wake up every day feeling grateful that you all are such a central part of my life.

Ron and Peggy Roloff, my father and mother—your compassion, love, tenderness, and toughness helped get me through the tough times and helped set a foundation for me.

My brothers and sister, Josh, Sam, and Ruth—thanks for putting up with me all those years, teaching me so much about life and being a source of support.

To Grandma and Grandpa Trice—for all the prayers, the love, the hospital visits, and the never ending support and encouragement. You are a great example of loving God and loving your children and grandchildren. What an example of living straight ahead for Jesus!

Thanks to the friends who have always encouraged me to keep reaching beyond life's minimums:

- Eric Jones—My best man and close friend
- Mike Jackson—Kept me going during those tough teenage years
- Gary Garbarino—Loyal to the end
- Dick Mann—Provided invaluable advice and input for this book, and whose mature counsel guides me often
- Greg "Bigfoot" Smith—Who believes in me and my ideas
- Gary Medlock—Rock-solid friendship
- Joe Lurker—Wise counselor and friend who guided me through several career decisions
- Terry Row—Teaches me to enjoy the finer things in life: birds, stars, chess, classical music
- Sammy—My loyal assistant and friend
- Jon Andreasen—Believed in me and taught me how to succeed

Thanks also to those people who have made a difference in my life in so many ways:

- Floyd and Jeanie Kvamme—Gave me the most significant break of my life
- To the school teachers whose patience and faith in me—even when I underachieved—made such a difference in shaping my attitudes.
- To Billy Barty for having the vision to start Little People of America, and to all the volunteers who keep it thriving in its mission to serve little people everywhere.
- To all the people who helped me build my farm and reality out of my visions and dreams.

I'd like to thank the American people for their understanding of and accommodations for little people and others with disabilities. Thanks to the United States Congress for the Americans with Disabilities Act.

Special thanks to those who, when faced with a choice between ending a pregnancy through abortion and bringing those like me and others with disabilities into the world, choose life. Your decision has enabled many to recognize the value of every human life, even those affected by physical disabilities.

Special thanks to the people at Multnomah Publishers for your patience and guidance in making this book a reality for me. Thanks to Tracy Sumner for turning my disjointed ramblings into a coherent life story, and to Jeff Gerke for his patience with me in putting the final polish on the project. Thanks to Don Jacobson, publisher and president of Multnomah, for his vision for the project, and to Ken Ruettgers for being a calming influence for me during the entire process.

Thanks to my employer, Clarify, Inc., one of the fastest-growing service software companies, whose vision has included me and given me the space for many achievements, including this book.

Last and most important, thanks to the Lord Jesus Christ, who gives me life and who enabled me to see past my disability to become all that I could.

PROLOGUE
LIFE ON THE FARM

I had a hunch.

It was March 3, 1990, a rainy morning in northwestern Oregon. I had just quit the best job I'd ever had—designing software in Silicon Valley. I was twenty-eight. My wife was six months pregnant with twins. We'd just bought a new house in Portland.

Yet here I was in Helvetia, Oregon, staring at a beat-up old farmhouse. Me and my hunch.

The house we'd just put earnest money on was new. This one was a dump. The first house was on a tiny lot. This one was on thirty-four acres. This one sat at the end of a gravel road, secluded amidst gently rolling hills and a patchwork of crops. This one boasted an overgrown peach orchard, crying for care, a ramshackle old barn, and a giant walnut tree just begging for a tire swing.

No joke: the house was really a dump. The rooms were filled with trash. The paint was peeling. The roof leaked. But I knew this place could be fixed up. What a place to raise kids! Every day they would have this fantastic playground out their back door. I had plans. I had a vision.

I had a hunch.

Now when you reach the end of that quarter-mile gravel road, you'll see an altogether different farm. The rustic barn has been restored almost board by board, given a new stone foundation, and painted red and white to give it that "Americana" look. The orchard is well kept and productive. In the summer it yields some of the biggest, sweetest peaches in the area. The farmhouse is a warm, beautiful home now—with a few special modifications.

But you'd probably not even notice these things because of what else you'd see. In the middle of the pond near the house is a thirty-foot pirate ship, the *Rolly Polly*. She boasts three sails, belowdecks quarters for captain and crew, and a bonafide plank.

Not far from the *Rolly Polly* is an Old West town. There's a blacksmith's shop to shoe your horses, a post office to handle your mail, a general store, a bank, and a jail to put bad guys in. The buildings are all mounted on skids, so the town can be rearranged at will. At the outskirts of town, there's even real tumbleweed. Unbeknownst to the average sheriff, three hundred feet of secret tunnels run underneath the town.

Remember when I said I had plans?

When you're ready for a break from the wild west, you can head over to the four-level tree house. It rises thirty-five feet between the branches of a sturdy old oak tree. The tree house is designed so it will sway in the wind but still be safe. There are six ways to get inside including stairs, a rope ladder, and a cargo net. The top section of the tree house is a hammock cabin with a grass roof. The verandah gives a panoramic view of the farm.

Beneath the restored barn is a seventy-foot underground mine shaft for the prospector who's feeling lucky. The barn itself contains a rec room with a big screen TV and a juice bar for neighborhood kids. Elsewhere on the property there's a 180-foot cable slide, a putting green, a soccer field, eight bridges (I love bridges), and numerous developed camping areas.

There's more on the drawing board, too. My next project is The Tower of Terror, a twenty-four-foot tower designed to shake, rattle, and roll anyone brave enough to climb to the top. It's for kids (and their more timid parents), so of course it will be completely safe.

Why have I built all this? To prove something? To show off? No. I've done it because I thought it would be fun—for my kids and for me. The writer of Ecclesiastes was right when he said there is a time for tears and a time for laughter. Considering the pain I've had in my life, I think it's high time to laugh.

So I built a Tom Sawyer adventure land. But it's not open for business. It's just imagination space for family and friends.

This farm is one testimony to the world that you can make something great out of what most people consider little.

LIVING—AND LOVING— LIFE WITH A DISABILITY

P eople look at me and assume I can't possibly be happy. I know some of them wonder how I deal with my disabilities, how I get around and function in a world that wasn't designed to accommodate "my kind." They want to hear the story about the little guy who overcame tremendous pain, setbacks, and prejudice to become a success. They want to know how I've "survived."

If I were on the outside looking at my life, I'd wonder the same things. But I haven't just "survived." On the contrary, I've thrived. I'm happy, content, and couldn't be more pleased with the experiences I've had.

I have lived every day of my life with what almost any person would consider a devastating physical disability, a disability that is immediately obvious when you see me.

I am, in politically correct terms, a little person. In other words, a dwarf. I am what in medical circles is called a diastrophic dwarf, meaning I am not only short in stature—I stand four feet, two inches tall—but I also have severe problems in my legs, knees, hips, shoulders, arms, and the rest of my body that make it impossible for me to stand up straight or walk without the aid of crutches.

My joints, including those in my hands and feet, are very visibly deformed. My hips and knees are a mess. Instead of the ball and socket joint that is in most people's hips, mine are more like a wishbone. One hip has two ball joints, and the other has no socket. There's a protrusion in one of my hips that keeps it from rotating properly. In addition, my arms and legs are abnormally short for my size. My doctors tell me they could do some radical corrective surgery to improve some of those problems. It's something for me to think about. However, after what I've been through, I'm in no rush to see the inside of any operating rooms.

There's no question about it: I stand out in a crowd. If you were to spend any time with me in public—in a shopping mall, in a restaurant, even in church—you'd feel the eyes looking my direction, especially the eyes of children, who, in their innocence, will simply stare at something greatly different from what they are used to seeing. That doesn't bother me, though. I know I'm different from other people, and I understand why someone would want to look at me. In fact, I'm more than willing to talk to people—especially kids—and answer questions about my condition.

I am one of roughly twenty-five thousand little people living in the United States today. Not all of us have the kinds of physical problems associated with my type of dwarfism. While not all little people consider themselves disabled, I do. There are more than a hundred types of dwarfism, and each type has its own set of physical challenges and issues. Some are, other than their lack of height, as healthy as anyone else. One example is my wife, Amy, who is an achondroplastic dwarf. She is short-statured like me, but otherwise completely healthy.

I spent much of my time as a child in hospitals, undergoing surgeries, going through incredibly painful rehabilitation, and withstanding more isolation than any child should have to endure. I spent literally years of my childhood in a hospital. The doctors and surgeons who worked with me performed every manner of procedure they knew—and many they didn't know—trying to correct the problems I had in my joints and bones. All of that for relatively little gain.

When the procedures were finished and I'd completed my rehabilitation, I still walked only with the aid of crutches. With the exception of only a few times in my life, I've always walked with my "sticks." I need my crutches to get around to this day, and I expect one day I will be confined to a wheelchair. Even now, I must use an electric cart in places like shopping malls and airports.

When I talk about those things, it might sound like I'm complaining or looking for pity because of the difficulties I've endured. I don't have time to think in those terms. I wouldn't waste the energy. I'm much too busy to worry about what I don't have or what could have been. Besides, you might be surprised at just how fast a guy on crutches can move. Imagine a low center of gravity and arms that have done the work of legs for years.

I'M LOVING LIFE

If I were to tell you everything about myself except my physical infirmities, you might think me the luckiest man in the world. You'd be right! I've had great success in my professional field—I sell multimillion-dollar computer systems. I have a happy marriage and four wonderful, healthy children. I have family and friends with whom I share great love. I live in one of the most beautiful areas of the United States—the Pacific Northwest—on a farm I have made both functional and fun.

Some people might look at me and think of the old cliché, "When life gives you lemons, make lemonade." It's true, I've enjoyed a great life despite—and I hesitate to use the word *despite*—my physical disability. But I don't look at the way I've been made as "lemons" at all. I won't make excuses or let my physical condition keep me from enjoying the things other people enjoy or keep me from excelling in whatever I choose to pursue. In fact, I think my condition has actually *enhanced* my life.

It's been said that when people lose their sight, their other senses become sharper, adapting to the loss of the one sense by expanding others. That's what's happened in my life. My short stature and physical infirmities have helped me develop in ways I'm sure I wouldn't have had I been average-sized and healthy.

I learned early that people react differently to me than they do to others. So I tried to learn how to leverage these reactions for my benefit. For example, I believe my disability has forced me to develop the people skills—the ability to communicate with and influence people—I've needed to be successful in my field of work. That has been my way of adapting to my world. Being little has forced me to stretch and strengthen "muscles" I wouldn't necessarily have exercised if I had been average-sized.

This might sound crazy, but I wouldn't want things any other way.

To someone who hasn't walked in my shoes, my disabilities look devastating. I can't tell you how many older women have passed me, lifted their hand to their mouths, and said, "Oh, my goodness, that's terrible. Look at that poor little boy." As many times as I heard that, it could've affected my self-esteem—if I'd let it.

My disabilities look like reason enough for me to focus on mere "survival." To me, however, they are simply part of everyday life. They are part of what has made me what I am. For that reason, I like the way I'm made.

GOING ABOVE AND BEYOND

I've never looked at my physical condition as a difficulty or trial. I've always thought it's up to me to get out of life all I can make of it.

I've had to adapt to the world around me while doing even the most mundane daily activities such as driving, going grocery shopping with my wife, or even changing my socks. But it hasn't been a hindrance to anything I really wanted to do.

I understand I have certain limitations because of my size and condition. Obviously, I could never play professional basketball or football. I've had days when I felt bad about being little, when I wished I were average-sized. I can remember days like that when I was a kid. I just wanted to be like the rest of the kids at school. I wondered what it would be like to be tall, so I could play basketball or football like my friends could. I even prayed at bedtime that God would allow me to wake up tall and without disabilities. No, God didn't do that miracle. Every morning I was still a diastrophic dwarf.

When I was in high school, I gave a speech for my school's Optimist Club. I titled the speech, "I See a Promise for Tomorrow." I talked about the social and technological changes in our society that are helping to make life better for disabled or handicapped people. I talked about what I saw as real advantages to being a little person. I wanted everyone who heard that speech to know I had accepted myself as I was made, and that I wouldn't change anything, even if I could.

I never wanted anyone to look at me and say, "He's done well for someone with those kinds of disabilities," or "He's pretty successful for a little person," or "He survived." I want to be able to look at my life and say I've made the best of my talents, period. I want people to see me as someone who reaches beyond what a lot of people in my position might reach for. I want people to think of me as someone who does all he can to rise above the expectations placed on him.

Many people with disabilities are too much into just getting by. They live down to the lowered expectations the world puts on them, or they use their problems as excuses not to go out and live to their potential. They let their problems determine what their lives are going to be. In other words, they allow their circumstances to dictate to them what they can and can't do.

I've known many people like that, and it breaks my heart—and angers me—when I see all that wasted potential. I believe there isn't a person around who doesn't have something that could keep him from living up to his potential. Think about that for a minute: All of us have some kind of hardship that could keep us from accomplishing great things. For me, it's my physical deformity. For someone else, it could be a rough family life that wounded his or her self-esteem. For still another person, it could be the lack of a formal education.

What I want to say in this book is that you don't have to let your circumstances—physical or otherwise—keep you from the good life. I believe you can still be a success despite whatever limitations your circumstances may put on you.

I've lived my life according to some core values my mother and father taught me from the time I could understand what they were saying. These values—compassion, hard work, devotion to family, personal character, faith in and love for God, and perseverance—have made me not only a happy man, but successful in almost anything I've undertaken. I want you to see how those things have worked in my life, and I want you to know it isn't just little people who have to think and act positively.

BRINGING ME
AND MY BROTHERS
INTO THE WORLD

I magine the shock and disappointment you would feel if you suddenly learned your baby, because of a genetic fluke, had been born with a severe physical disability—one that would always be a part of his life, that made you wonder how he would get by as an adult, that made you question if your child could survive in this world, that would require your child to undergo many painful surgeries and subsequent rehabilitation.

Imagine the shock of knowing your child was like me: not just a dwarf, but a dwarf with severe physical disabilities. What would it do to your heart and mind knowing your flesh and blood would have to endure daily pain and be ostracized from many of life's activities?

Now add two more children with such abnormalities, including one with an irreparable heart condition that made his first birthday a miracle. Would you ask, "Why us? What have we done wrong to deserve this?" Would you look at your life and wonder if there was any sense, any reason to it? Would you wish you could trade lives with somebody else?

It is hard to imagine this scenario taking place in the life of one couple, but it has. It happened to a couple I know quite well: Ron and Peggy Roloff, my parents.

When I think about situations in which the right people were put in the right place for one special purpose, I think about my parents. They were a perfect fit for one of the most difficult sets of parenting problems any couple could face. Not only did they have my problems to deal with, but also those of my brother Joshua (who was born with severe heart and lung problems and has only through a medical miracle lived to his mid-thirties) and my youngest brother Samuel, another diastrophic dwarf.

Of my parents' four children, only my sister, Ruth, had no physical abnormalities. Ruth, the eldest, has grown to a statuesque five feet ten and is completely healthy. The three boys, however, underwent a combined thirty-six surgeries, as well as incredible amounts of recovery time and physical therapy.

Samuel and I each spent literally years of our childhood in the hospital undergoing all sorts of procedures that were attempts to correct problems associated with diastrophic dwarfism. But we had it easy compared with Joshua, who has been at death's doorstep more times than Mom and Dad can remember. Joshua has lived each day of his life knowing it could very easily be his last, that his frail, damaged heart could give out for the final time.

WITHOUT WARNING

There's an old saying, "Forewarned is forearmed." There can be great value in knowing when tough times are headed your way. There was nothing, though, that could have prepared my parents for the trauma that was the day of my birth.

Ruth was less than a year old when Mom found out she was pregnant with me. Mom and Dad greeted the news of my pending arrival joyfully. Mom's pregnancy with me was fairly normal. There was a little more amniotic fluid than is typical, but the doctors told Mom and Dad this was possibly a symptom of twins and nothing to worry about. An Xray showed that everything—as far as the doctors knew—was normal, although the doctors believed I might arrive a few weeks prematurely.

Mom went into labor with me early in the morning of October 7, 1961. She, Dad, and Ruth got in our 1948 DeSoto and headed for Children's Hospital in San Francisco. If you've ever seen a '48 DeSoto, you know they're large and bulky, and built much like a tank on four wheels. It takes a lot to damage a DeSoto. It's a good thing, too, because on the way to the hospital, another driver ran a stop sign and smashed into the side of the car.

The DeSoto's body was dented, but the car was drivable. Mom was jarred a bit, but not hurt. Ruth, who was sixteen months old and sitting in the seat between our parents, was thrown into Mom by the force of the collision and was fine (there were no seat belts in cars in 1948). The other car was demolished.

Dad got out and quickly exchanged information with the other driver, who wasn't injured. "I can't stay here," Dad said. "I have to get my wife to the hospital. Just call the police because we have to go." They dropped Ruth off at Mom's aunt's home on the way to the hospital. Finally, around seven in the morning, Dad checked Mom into Children's Hospital.

Fathers weren't allowed in delivery rooms back then. So, after getting Mom checked into the hospital, Dad left to take care of some business. By then, Mom's labor pains had stopped, she says because of the accident.

By noon the pains started again and not long afterwards I was born. Dad saw Mom in the recovery room, smiled, and told her, "This builds character." They both waited for someone to bring me to them so they could hold me and celebrate the birth of their first son.

That was when things at Children's Hospital took a strange—almost nightmarish—turn.

WHERE'S MY BABY?

Mom saw me very briefly in the delivery room moments after I was born, but it never occurred to her that there was anything wrong with me. To this day, she remembers thinking how compact I looked for a newborn, how I didn't have what she calls "the usual spider monkey look" of a newborn baby. She remembers thinking how I resembled my father, with a very prominent—actually, the word she uses is "big"—nose. I was a big baby: eight pounds, eight ounces, and nineteen inches long.

The delivery room staff pointed out to her that my feet turned in, and a nurse touched one of my feet to her face. Mom remembers thinking my feet looked cute, not realizing they were deformed.

With that, I was whisked out of the room. Mom was told she would be able to see me in a few hours. They finished the routine medical work on Mom, then took her to her room, where they made sure she stayed in bed. After undergoing something as traumatic as childbirth, it would seem logical that a woman could get to sleep. But Mom couldn't. All she could think about was holding her newborn son. That chance wasn't going to come for some time.

Mom waited and waited, ringing the buzzer on her bed to get a nurse's attention so they could bring her son to her. "We'll check on it," she was told, only to hear nothing from anyone. Dad and Ruth came into Mom's room, and she told them, "They haven't brought the baby in. I haven't seen him yet. What's happening?"

By this time, Mom was in tears and near panic. Dad went to check on the newborns, but when he looked in the nursery window, he couldn't see the name Roloff anywhere. I was literally being hidden from view. He returned to Mom's room, knowing something was wrong. But he didn't let on to Mom. He just kissed her and went to take Ruth. Mom continued to wait.

The truth was the doctors didn't know how to handle the situation. They didn't want to tell my parents I was deformed because they feared what my parents might do. They had no idea what Mom's reaction would be. Would she abandon me? Refuse to care for me? Such things had been known to happen. So they spent hours consulting with one another about how to break the news to my parents about what was wrong with me.

The problem was the doctors didn't *know* what was wrong with me. They looked at my stubby arms and legs, my malformed hands and feet, and the other deformities in my little body; and they knew I was deformed, but they couldn't name my condition. None of them had seen anything like this before. Doctors are now more familiar with dwarfism, but back then few had seen it.

You have to remember this was 1961. There was no way for expectant parents to know their child would be a dwarf, so whenever it happened, it was a shock. As far as my parents knew, I was going to be just like my sister Ruth: healthy, normal, and ready to grow to average size. However, back then—unlike today, when dwarfism can be detected with prenatal testing—there was a certain percentage of dwarf children born to average-sized parents. It was, and still is, a shock for parents to find out their child is a dwarf.

While the doctors struggled over how to handle this situation, Mom and Dad waited and worried. Finally, my father forced their hand.

BRING HIM TO US—NOW!

Around nine the night of my birth, Mom tried to call Dad at home. But the switchboard operator told her no outgoing calls were allowed at night. Mom began crying and pleading with the operator to allow the call to go through. The call went through. She told Dad she still hadn't seen me or been told anything.

Dad had heard enough. He and Ruth got in the slightly damaged DeSoto and headed back to the hospital. Dad was determined to have answers, and he was going to get them *now*.

Dad walked into the hospital, marched to the maternity ward, saw the doctors hovering around, and demanded to know why neither he nor Mom had been allowed to see me. The doctors wouldn't tell him anything, but he could see concern in their eyes. I think Dad kind of snapped. He raged at the doctors in attendance, "You have one minute to have that baby with his mother, or I'm charging you with kidnapping."

I don't know if a charge of kidnapping would have held any water in a situation like that, but someone got the message. Within a few minutes, a young nurse brought me—wrapped up like a little mummy—to Mom.

Mom has told me that her first thought when she saw me was that I was fine. She thought I was a healthy baby who just needed a little extra medical attention. "He's fine!" she said. "I was so worried." But there was still something strange going on.

The young nurse, after handing me to my mother, left the room but quickly returned. "I'm not supposed to leave you alone with the baby," she said, adding that they wanted to keep me wrapped up until the doctors talked to them.

Finally, one of the hospital's pediatricians came in to explain what was wrong with me—at least what he knew. "Well, I need to tell you about the baby," he said, the look on his face telling my mother that it was something serious. "His feet are turned in. It's called clubfoot." Mom had no idea what that meant. "And his arms are short. It's not just a hand coming straight off his shoulder or anything, but his arms are very short."

They unwrapped me to show her what the doctor was talking about, but Mom still didn't understand what was wrong with me. She could see that my feet were turned in and my arms and legs were a little short, but it seemed odd to her that the doctor would paint a picture of a deformed baby. She just looked at me, thinking how I was an adorable little boy.

My mother and I stayed in the hospital for a few more days while specialists examined me to determine what was wrong. On my birth certificate, they put the word *achondroplasia*, a condition that is caused by a gene mutation that affects growth, especially in the long bones—such as those in the arms and legs.

I was six years old before I was diagnosed correctly as a diastrophic dwarf. In 1961 they knew very little about the many variations of dwarfism. The first person to tell Mom I was a dwarf was a physical therapist who was working on me. Mom asked her, "Why do you think his arms and legs are so short?" The therapist told her I was a dwarf and that short arms and legs were normal for a dwarf. Mom was shocked almost to the point of fainting. She knew nothing about dwarfism. Her first thoughts when she heard the word "dwarf" was of a troll under a bridge.

The therapist gave my mother information about Little People of America, a nonprofit organization that provides support and information to little people and their families, and my parents looked into it. They learned much about dwarfism from LPA—and since then, from raising me.

As my parents learned more about my condition, they began to despair as they faced heavy life questions. Parents always wonder what their child will become once he grows up, but for someone with my condition, the questions become all the more difficult. My parents didn't wonder *what* I would do, *what kind* of woman I'd marry, or *how many* grandchildren I would one day father for them. They wondered *if* I could do any of those things. They wondered how I could function as a little person in a world that was designed by and for average-sized people. They wondered what I could do for a living, if I could ever marry, and if I could have children.

But I wasn't going to be my parents' only disabled child. Their second son, Joshua, was born with a condition that made mine seem almost minor.

JOSH—THE *REAL* MIRACLE

When Joshua was born—about two weeks before Christmas in 1964, when I was over two years old—my parents faced more childbirth trauma. Only this time it was the uncertainty over whether their new baby would ever make it out of the hospital alive. Not long after the delivery, the doctors diagnosed Josh as having severe heart and lung problems they thought would probably take his life before he was a day old.

"I wouldn't even name him," one doctor told my mother. Mom and Dad did name him, and Joshua didn't die. Two days before Christmas, Joshua came home.

Three and a half decades after his birth, my brother Joshua is alive and enjoying life. He lives on my parents' property in California in his own cottage. He has undergone several major surgeries, some by doctors who believed they could correct his condition, only to find out that his condition couldn't be corrected. He underwent another surgery to repair a brain abscess, and it was a miracle he lived through that. He also has scoliosis, a condition his doctors say could make it even more difficult for his heart and lungs to function as it worsens. He is faced with a true dilemma: He can risk his life undergoing corrective surgery for the scoliosis, or he can face eventual death as his spine curves more, making it harder for him to breathe.

Josh loves life and appreciates every day he is given. It's no wonder he's like that since it is truly a miracle he has lived as long as he has. He's had many close calls with death, and Mom has had to resuscitate him more times than she cares to remember. Many times Josh's heart and lungs have simply stopped functioning on their own, and on other occasions he's had seizures that would have taken his life had someone not been there to help him.

But Josh is tough. In fact, people who know him think he's the toughest guy on the planet. We have a running joke in our family that Josh will probably outlive us all.

Joshua is like my dad in that he loves people. He's very friendly, outgoing, and—although he has a soft voice—talkative and thoughtful. My kids love their Uncle Josh, and it is always a joy to see them interact with him when he comes to visit us. We treasure the times he's able to come up to Oregon and stay with us for extended periods. He is such a help to me around the farm, helping with mowing, pruning, feeding the cows, and whatever else needs to be done.

Joshua has always been an encouragement to me and the rest of the family. His condition is incurable and terminal; each breath he takes could be his last. Perhaps because of this, he approaches life as something to be treasured.

THREE IS ENOUGH

After Joshua was born, my parents decided Mom's childbearing days were over. They figured that they had three children, two of them severely disabled, and that was enough for any couple to bear. But, as Mom points out every time she talks about it, God had another plan.

We were living in Concord, California, when Mom discovered she was again pregnant. Mom and Dad had used birth control after Joshua's birth, so they were confident there wouldn't be another addition to the family. Surprise!

Almost immediately, the news of Mom's pregnancy was met with comments like, "Why would you want to have more children?" People suggested she get an abortion rather than face the possibility of having another disabled child. Mom wouldn't do it, though. To her, this child would be as much a blessing from God as the previous three had been, and she knew there was no way she would give him or her up.

The doctors told Mom that she had almost no chance of having another dwarf child, that it just didn't happen. It was a one-in-a-million thing, they said. What they didn't know—what no one knew back then—was that diastrophic dwarfism runs in families. In fact, the latest statistics say that the siblings of a diastrophic dwarf have a twenty-five percent chance of being diastrophics themselves.

Mom believed she was going to have a little girl, whom she would name Sarah, who would be average-sized. She was wrong on both counts. She gave birth to her third boy, and it was immediately obvious that he was a dwarf. He had the same kinds of physical characteristics I had: short limbs and deformed joints.

Mom and Dad knew they would have a challenging life together raising me. When Josh came along, they could see it was going to be even tougher. But when Sam was born, everybody close to the family knew it was going to be an incredible ride for the six of us.

That it was!

THE RIGHT PEOPLE
FOR A TOUGH JOB

Raising three boys as physically messed up as we were isn't something just any married couple could've done. It was something that required superhuman love, patience, compassion, strength, firmness, gentleness, faith, and wisdom.

Neither of my parents is a little person. In fact, I doubt if either had ever *known* a dwarf before I was born. They were both healthy, strong, and tall, so they had no points of reference for what they would face in raising us. It was all on-the-job training. But they not only *survived* the ordeal, they *excelled*.

My folks cared for our physical needs, loved us, gave us direction, and got tough with us when we needed it. They prepared us for life in a world that doesn't cater to those with our kinds of disabilities. I can say with absolute certainty that I would not be where I am today without what my parents did for me.

I've never lost sight of what Mom and Dad endured and sacrificed for my brothers and me. All while still caring for a daughter who needed attention, too. We couldn't have had better parents. Many people might have broken down under considerably less stress than what my folks endured. Frankly, I don't know how they handled it without breaking down emotionally or mentally.

Through all the pain and challenges we faced, Mom and Dad taught us that we had as much chance to be happy as anyone else, that it was our attitude, our approach to life, and our faith in God that would determine what we would do in our lives and how happy we would be.

DAD: TOUGH, YET TENDER

When I'm asked about the people in my life I most respect and admire, my first thoughts are always of my father. A man of extraordinary conviction (real hard headed and opinionated, like me), strength, and character; this tough guy ex-Marine is also a man with amazing love, compassion, and tenderness for people. He's John Wayne-tough and Jimmy Stewart-tender. He's a man whose purpose in life is to glorify God in all he does, and he's not ashamed to tell anybody who will listen.

Dad doesn't just love people; he enjoys them. He truly likes being around people, talking with people, helping them out. He is the kind of person who stands up for the downtrodden or disadvantaged, who talks with the lonely, offers the hungry a meal, the thirsty a drink, and the tired and cold a warm bed to sleep in. He never does it out of some sense of duty, either. He truly wants to help people out in any way he can, and he isn't hung up on social position, race, or religious beliefs.

He is without fear or prejudice. He and Mom spent time in the Watts neighborhood of Los Angeles, a fairly dangerous area back in the eighties, doing Christian ministry for the people in the area. To him, a person's skin color or economic place in the world means nothing. I can tell you that if you put my father in a social situation in which someone was uncomfortable or feeling left out, Dad would find him and make him feel welcomed and important.

But there is a side to Dad that seems almost contradictory. It's a part of him that can come out when he feels his loved ones or people who can't fend for themselves are threatened.

WILLING TO CONFRONT

Dad is very much into loving God and people, but he still has a little of the United States Marine Corps and a little bit of the street fighter in him. He isn't a brawler by any means, but when people get picked on because they are smaller, weaker, or can't fend for themselves, Dad is more than willing to get physical.

Dad isn't an exceptionally big man—five feet eleven inches tall—but he's pretty well built, and he is one of the most determined people I've ever known. He wouldn't back down from anyone or anything if he felt there was an injustice being done. We saw him in a lot of scuffles and scrapes over the years, many he might well have avoided.

One memorable confrontation took place in Santa Cruz, where Dad was taking all of us to the beach one sunny northern California day. We had our swimming trunks, our inner tubes, and our picnic basket with us. It was going to be one of the many great expeditions Dad took us on.

On the way to the beach, we stopped at a light, where a man in the car next to us started a profanity-laced tirade at his wife. They were in a convertible, so we could hear every word he said. After listening to that for a minute, Dad exploded out of the car and told the man he didn't appreciate him using that kind of language to his wife or in front of us. Naturally, the man in the convertible didn't respond positively.

A few minutes later Dad came back to the car and calmly said, "Can you believe that guy? What a knucklebrain. He'll think twice before swearing like that in front of my family." Then we headed off for our fun day at the beach.

Many times I saw Dad confront—and intimidate—doctors he felt were giving him the runaround when my brothers and I were getting worked on. I saw him get in the face of my high school gym teacher—a strict, ex-Marine himself—after I told him the teacher insisted I change into gym shorts for PE every day, despite the fact that changing was a major undertaking for me.

I can remember Dad storming into the front office at school and demanding to see the teacher right away. When the teacher got there, Dad opened fire. "For sixteen years Matt has had to wear braces on his legs every day and night," he said. "Now that he doesn't have to wear those stinking things anymore, he can wear anything he wants. Is that clear?"

Some of Dad's most heated confrontations were with the Internal Revenue Service. Unless you want to start a long, one-sided conversation, it's still not a good idea to bring up the IRS with my dad. Dad reasoned that if he was going to keep his three disabled children at home so he and Mom could care for us—rather than turning them over to the government—he should be entitled to a few tax breaks. The logic is simple: He would actually be saving the government money by caring for his kids himself, so the IRS should allow him to keep some of his earnings in order to care for them.

Dad wrote off everything even remotely related to caring for us. He wrote off his mileage to and from hospitals, medical therapy, counseling. He'd write off meals he'd pay for on the way to or from the hospital. If he could in any way associate something with our disabilities, he'd write it off.

Every year he sent in his federal tax return with all the deductions, and almost every year he got audited. Nine audits. One year, when the local IRS office called to inform him of the audit, the officer asked him to come to the office for the audit. "No, I can't do that," Dad said. "I'm working ninety hours a week and taking care of three handicapped kids. I don't have time to come to your office. If you want to audit me, you come to my house."

"Mr. Roloff, we can't do that."

"Well, then you can't audit me," he said, the tone in his voice more than suggesting that he was in command of the situation. "If you want to audit me, you come to my house. Period."

Eventually, the auditors came to the house. Dad was polite to them. He led them into his office and invited them to sit down…in the wheelchairs he had set up in advance. Then he brought us boys in, so the agents could see that we were, in fact, quite disabled. He then produced all his receipts. He had a receipt and a rationale for every one of his deductions, and he painstakingly explained each one to the agents. No question was left unanswered. When the process was finished, the auditors didn't find anything inappropriate. Dad felt he had won a moral victory.

While I admire my father for so fearlessly taking on IRS audits, I realize those battles took a lot out of him. It was a battle every year to save just a few hundred dollars on his tax bill, and it seemed to me, sooner or later someone at the IRS would realize it just wasn't worth it to audit my dad. Here he was, a hardworking guy with three legitimately disabled kids, and the IRS wouldn't leave him alone. It wasn't like he wasn't paying his taxes, either. He was playing by their rules, only to have them audit him every year.

I think I came by a lot of my personality traits honestly. I am very people oriented, and I'll take the time to talk with anyone—have a cup of coffee or a meal with anyone I meet. Like Dad, I'm also a battler, a trait that got me in a little trouble at times when I was younger. Like Dad, I've also mellowed, realizing I need to pick my battles. More than all that, though, I think I'm like Dad in that a lot of my personality traits were forged in the fire of adversity.

A TOUGH BACKGROUND

If you want to know what made my Dad so tender, compassionate, and tough, you need look no further than his own youth. Dad understands all too well what it is like to be down and out because he has been there himself. When he was five years old, his alcoholic mother left him and his siblings on a street corner in San Francisco and boarded a bus, leaving his father as the only parent. Dad had to fend for himself much of the time while his father worked.

Dad learned how to fight and scrap just to survive in a world not made for kids on their own. He had nothing then, and he had little hope of ever having anything. It was a tough childhood, but it made him determined not to let the same thing happen to his children, if he ever had any. It also made him compassionate toward those in the same position he once was in himself.

THE BEGINNING OF A VITAL UNION

Mom and Dad came from such completely opposite backgrounds that it's a wonder they ever met, let alone dated, got married, and had four children. While Dad grew up basically parentless, Mom lived under a roof with her mother and father who cared for her—pampered her, the way she describes it. It was the epitome of a stable family life. While Dad had to be tough and wily just to survive, life had been pretty easy for Mom. All through high school, Dad was a star athlete. Mom, on the other hand, was the girl always in the middle of the social events.

Dad and Mom first met because my grandmother (Mom's mom) frequently invited him to Sunday dinner. Dad came into contact with Grandma through church, and for some reason only she knew at the time, she took a liking to him. She loved my father from the time she met him, and since she knew Dad was alone a lot she would invite him over.

He came to the dinners, all the time keeping an eye on my mother. At first, she wouldn't have anything to do with Ron Roloff. After all, he just wasn't in her social class. Eventually, through some kind of minor miracle, these two teens from different worlds fell in love and were married.

Together they embarked on an adventurous life, a life filled with genuine difficulties and heartache. A life in which both would feel despair, shed tears, and be pushed mentally, physically, and spiritually to their absolute limits.

A CHILDHOOD PRISON

S tarting when I was less than a year old, I was in and out of hospitals almost constantly. First at the Shriners Hospital in San Francisco, then later at a private hospital when my family got medical insurance that would cover my condition.

When I wasn't in a hospital, I was either getting ready to go or recovering from my last stay. I'm not talking about hospital stays of a few days or even a few weeks. I'm talking about months at a time. I'm talking about days and weeks on end when I would hardly see my parents or any of my family. I'm talking about feelings of isolation so intense that I wondered if I'd ever be allowed to see my family or friends again. It was literally like being in prison. I remember being put in before Thanksgiving one year and not getting out until months into the next year. For a kid, a two-month-long stay in a hospital is an eternity—especially over Christmas.

The surgeries and procedures I endured were attempts to correct—or at least improve—the conditions in my joints and bones. While orthopedic problems are common in little people, not all dwarfs have them to the extent I do. My wife never had any physical problems even remotely as serious as mine. My brother Sam had some of the same kinds of problems I had, but they were not as severe.

A prominent doctor with Shriners once said of me, "Matt was one of the most corrected individuals in Shriners' history." I had surgeries to straighten my knees and legs, and to straighten and strengthen my hips. I had follow-up surgeries, and surgeries to remove pins that had been placed in my bones to assist in healing. I don't even know exactly how many surgeries I had as a kid—between twenty and thirty.

I was something of a guinea pig back then. Many of the procedures the Shriners doctors tried on me were experimental, and some had never been tried. They wanted to do all kinds of procedures, and my parents, not knowing what could be done to help my condition, were willing to go with anything that might help. Some of the surgeries involved breaking, twisting, and straightening my bones, then setting them and putting me in a body cast. Some of the procedures were considered a success, while others turned out to be a waste of time. To this day, you can still find medical books and journals with accounts of the work that was done on me.

In addition to the surgeries, I underwent all sorts of therapies—some of them torturous—to straighten, twist, and lengthen different parts of my body. I remember one in particular that was an attempt to straighten my hips. It was performed on a little torture device called a butt strap, and it involved laying me out on my chest with a pillow under my knees and securing a large leather strap across my rear end and tightening it down. This went on for almost two months without much in the way of results.

KNOWING WHAT WAS COMING

In later stays, when my parents checked me into the hospital, I knew what was ahead for me. I had a diary back then, and I can remember writing in it one day when I was being checked into the hospital. I was issued my hospital clothing and taken to my room. That was when the loneliness set in. I took out my diary and wrote, "Lord, why is this happening to me?"

I was nine years old at the time, and I knew the kind of pain I was going to have to suffer, the isolation from my family and friends I would have to endure, and the confinement I would have to face.

Surgeries at the San Francisco Shriners Hospital were performed on Tuesdays and Thursdays. When they had a slot open for your surgery, you had to go because if you didn't, someone else certainly would. I was pretty much always on a waiting list for the surgeries the doctors felt I needed, and when Mom and Dad received a letter telling them a date was open for the surgery, I had to be ready to go.

When I was a small child, my family didn't have the kind of money or insurance that would have allowed us an alternative to Shriners, so we were forced to accept what Shriners offered. That put us—and many other families—over a barrel because when something is free, as Shriners is, it puts the caregiver in complete control of the situation. It's a take-it-or-leave-it proposition.

Mom and Dad once made the mistake of taking me to the hospital without telling me what was going on. After they admitted me, I was taken—kicking and screaming—into an isolation ward to get me calmed down. Mom and Dad thought I'd actually lost my mind.

After that, Dad would talk to me about staying there and undergoing surgery. "This is what the doctors think we should do, and we think we should do it, too," Dad would tell me. "You think about it." When it was put that way, something inside me told me that Dad wouldn't steer me wrong, that he had my best interests in mind. Of course, I never liked being in the hospital, and I certainly didn't like the surgeries or the rehabilitation, but I went willingly when Dad put it to me that way.

Sometimes, though, I felt so frustrated and in pain because of what was going on that I snapped at them. One time I screamed in my mother's face, "I *hate* you!"

Dad talked to me about it. "Matt," he said, "I know you don't hate your mother. She knows that, too. You hate the way things are now. Well, I hate this, too. I hate this situation. If there were anything I could do to change it, I would. But we have to get through these hard times together."

My first clear recollection of a long hospital stay occurred when I was five years old.

THE ISOLATION WARD

My mom and dad started talking to me about the pending stay several weeks before the check-in date. They even made me feel like I'd made the decision to go and have the painful surgery. I was a little scared but not much. I knew the routine, and although the first couple of days were going to be tough in getting to know the other kids in the ward, I knew I would soon make friends and might even have a little fun during my stay.

As my mom pulled up to the big fountain in front of the hospital, I took a deep breath of fresh air—knowing it would be my last for a while. We started through the check-in routine. I must've been a little nervous because I started chewing my fingernails. When the nurse saw me do it, she immediately accused me of having pinworms. Grounds for isolation.

The nurse whispered something in my mother's ear. I didn't like the look on my mother's face, and I especially didn't like where this was going.

My mother said the tearful good-bye and left. Instead of taking me to the regular ward with the other children, I was taken straight to an isolation cubicle—an eight-by-ten room with a bed, a small table, and a toilet.

"Why are you taking me in here?" I asked the nurse.

"We need to put you by yourself for a few days in case you have pinworms."

"But I don't," I protested. I knew I didn't.

"Well, just to make sure, you'll be in here a few days."

It was more like weeks.

SOME PAINFUL—AND VIVID—MEMORIES

I'm amazed now at how much of my time in the hospital I remember. Some of my most vivid memories are of the things inside the Shriners Hospital. I can remember the colors in my room and in the hallways, the smells you associate with a hospital. I can remember the faces of the people—the patients, the doctors, the nurses, the parents who visited. All of those things seem as fresh in my mind today as they were the day I left.

One particularly unpleasant memory was the physical pain. You have to realize that the surgeries done on me involved opening me up, breaking and cutting and rearranging my bones, closing me up, then putting me in a body cast so my bones would heal straight.

I can remember waking up in such pain I couldn't think straight. I just wanted it to go away. Like any kid, I hated needles, but after some of the surgeries I literally begged for shots of painkillers. "Please give me a shot!" But those had to be limited because they didn't want me to leave the hospital a drug addict. When they'd ask where I hurt, all I could tell them was "Everywhere!"

I remember a time when I was in such searing, relentless pain that I sincerely begged for someone to cut off my legs. To me, the thought of walking again didn't compare with the pain I felt. I wanted it gone, and I didn't care what it cost me.

Even though I was miserable in the hospital, I got through it. I survived it and got tougher and stronger because of it. I lived one day at a time, and I was able to pull myself together enough to make it.

That was something many of us at Shriners Hospital had to do. You see, there were many kids in there whose conditions were far worse than mine, conditions that meant a lifetime of disfigurement. I believe that is part of what has taught me to stay away from self-pity. I had friends who'd lost their legs and arms in accidents, kids who had been horribly disfigured and burned, boys and girls who had no hope of ever walking—with or without crutches. As much as I suffered in that hospital, there was always someone who had it worse than I did.

When I think back on those days, I realize that in another way I was one of the truly fortunate ones at that hospital.

FAMILY SUPPORT

From the time I was old enough to understand what was going on, there was one thing I always looked forward to when I was in the hospital: Mom and Dad's visits. There were few certainties in my young life, but one of them was that my parents would be there for me as much as possible—and as much as the hospital would allow.

The visitation system Shriners used back then was horrible, both for the children and for their parents. Parents could only visit their children once a week, and even at that they had only two hours to tend to all their business—talking to doctors, making appointments, signing papers, and so on—at the hospital. When the parents arrived at the hospital, they had to sit in the waiting room, where they were given a piece of paper with the patient's number on it. The parent would then wait to be called and led down the hall to the ward. The parent would spend his or her time with the child but had to leave in time to give the other parent a chance to visit.

Mom remembers spending her allotted time with me, then having to endure my crying and her own when she had to leave me. She remembers how heart-wrenching it was to walk down the hall away from my room, all the while hearing me crying for her to come back. Mom cried as she left me, wanting desperately to turn and come back to me, but she knew she couldn't come back. Not for another week.

There seemed to be an attitude among some of the staff at Shriners that once you dropped your child off, he was *theirs* and you no longer had any say in how he was cared for. And if you did anything that was perceived as disruptive or obstructive, there was a possibility you might be banned from seeing your child.

Mom remembers one time trying to comfort Sam, who was very little at the time. Sam was crying, and Mom tried to comfort him only to have one of the nurses come over, snatch him away, put him back in his bed, and say, "If you continue to make him cry, you can't come here anymore." Mom couldn't argue because she didn't want to be banned from the hospital.

The Shriners Hospital logic was that too much parental visitation would have been disruptive to the routine. They believed those kinds of disruptions had a detrimental effect on the workings in the hospital, the schedules, and the kids' emotions. They didn't want to have to deal with children who were upset and crying when their parents had to leave.

Although I missed being with my family terribly when I was in the hospital, I was, it turns out, one of the really fortunate few because my parents actually came to see me. It was a sad situation for many of the kids at Shriners. Many of them were simply dropped off there, and their parents or relatives rarely—if ever—came to visit them. I can still remember kids—some of whom were in far worse shape than I was—whose parents absolutely never visited them. They were, for all intents and purposes, abandoned at the hospital.

In fairness to many of those parents, you need to understand that Shriners was a charitable organization for people who might not otherwise be able to afford the kinds of treatment the kids got there. Many of the children came from distances that made it impossible for their parents—many of whom couldn't afford to take a day off work to come see them when the hospital allowed visitors—to visit them regularly.

My parents always thought it was sad to see these children without visitors, and oftentimes my dad, true to the way he is with people, would stop and take the time to chat with a kid whose Mom or Dad couldn't make it. Dad became something of a father figure to a lot of the kids whose parents didn't come. Not only did he visit me and my brother, he also—as much as the hospital would allow—took time to say hello to other kids and to give them some encouragement. They loved him.

I was doubly blessed because I had grandparents—my mom's mother and father—who loved me and would do whatever it took to get a chance to see me. Grandma and Grandpa would find a good vantage point outside my window, and Mom would pick me up and carry me to where they could see me. They would smile and wave at me, and I'd smile back. We had to do this quickly, though, because Mom knew she'd be asked to leave if one of the nurses walked in.

Grandma would come by the hospital nearly every day to drop something off—a little toy for me to play with or a book to read. Sometimes she'd come to my window where I could see her wave. If the curtains were open, she could actually talk to me through the glass.

We always had a lot of visitors when we were in the hospital, but because of the rules we had to be pretty clever about getting them to actually see us. It was important to my brother and me to have the kind of caring support system we had in our family. It was a touch point to the real world. We were never starved for the knowledge that there were people who loved us and wanted to see us. It was that support system that overcame some of the shortcomings in how the staff handled people, particularly the young patients.

THE NURSES

I remember my grandmother bringing me one of those little puzzles with the squares in a small frame. You had to move the squares around until you got the picture right. I loved those. I was so proud to have finished the superman picture, and I set the little puzzle on my window waiting for Grandmother's next visit.

The morning before that visit, the nurse walked in and said, "What's this?"

"My puzzle," I said. "I've just finished it and I'm going to show my grandmother."

She took the puzzle and scrambled it all up. "Now you can do it again," she said, smiling.

I was crushed. Today, thirty years later, I can still remember that hurt as clearly as the day it happened.

We had to deal with a lot of nurses at Shriners. I can remember how different the nurses were from one another: how we loved some of them, tolerated others, and despised a few. They had everything from the proverbial Nurse Ratched to Florence Nightingale at the hospital. Some of them were deeply compassionate and truly loved kids. We always loved having those nurses around. Others, though, seemed interested only in sticking with the hospital's routine, and they weren't about to let anything like concerned, sometimes heartsick, parents get in the way of a smoothly running children's hospital

The Shriners nurses were largely unyielding when it came to enforcing the visitation rules. My parents did all they could to get around the rules and see me more, but it wasn't easy. Mom remembers walking up to my hospital room's window and looking in to see me. When she saw me, she tapped on the window and waved at me, only to have the nurse give her a look and walk over and close the blinds.

One of the things the other patients and I regularly did at the hospital was check on the nurses' schedules to see who would be working on a given day. We were happy to see the names of some of them, disappointed to see others. It got to where we remembered their names and, more importantly to us, the way they treated us when they were working.

SOME POSITIVE CHANGES

I don't want to make it sound like Shriners Hospital was all bad or that my family is bitter about things that happened back then. They did a lot of things right. Tuesday night was Bingo night. Often they had clowns come in. They had movie nights in the miniature theater in the hospital. We had recreation hour. I'm grateful they tried to help me, and I recognize that Shriners has made even more improvements in how it handles people today.

I've had to put a lot of the things that happened to me into context, realizing that it was the sixties, and the medical community—including the charitable organizations such as Shriners—had much to learn about handling patients and their families. I believe the people at Shriners—the administration, the doctors, the nurses, and the rest of the staff—did what they thought would work best for the children in that situation. Unfortunately, the policies in place were being implemented by fallible human beings who had limited resources, and sometimes the results weren't what the families of the children would have wanted.

My parents felt the strain of those days. As a parent myself, I now have some small idea of how they must have felt. When I think about how I'd feel if even one of my kids had to go through something like that, I am all the more amazed that my parents got through it the way they did.

Mom admits that there were times when she wondered if she might break down. She talks now of a mental picture she would get when things got really tough. It was a picture of her walking precariously along the edge of a very steep precipice. When she got so emotionally, spiritually, and mentally exhausted, she wondered what would have been wrong with just going over the edge. But she remembers thinking how useless that would have been because all that would happen is that she would be put in an institution, put on medication, and made to get back up on the edge. In the long run, it just wasn't worth it to fall, so she decided to keep her balance—day by day.

It must do something to your sense of compassion to watch your children go through thirty-odd surgeries. It certainly had an effect on my father. He and Mom have had to go through my surgeries, Sam's surgeries, and Josh's surgeries, including one in which he was operated on for a brain abscess that could have—the doctors say *should* have—killed him. Enduring all that has made my father and mother more understanding, compassionate people.

Dad also grew real compassion for people who have to endure tough times because of physical infirmities. He has a heart for people who are hurting. Now, if he sees someone in a bank or a mall who is confined to a wheelchair, he'll always take time to talk to that person. He will ask the question most people wouldn't ask: "What happened to you?" Then, with his eyes fixed on that person's eyes, he'll listen. I think raising us boys—seeing us in wheelchairs, in body casts, and on crutches—gives him license to be that way.

My mother also did her share of growing. She became an amazingly strong woman, a woman who now speaks at seminars and other women's gatherings and who makes regular radio appearances to talk about her experiences and how they have helped her grow as a woman of God and as a person.

In addition to her strength, my mother's love and compassion is amazing. When you meet her, you can feel the love and warmth coming from her just because you are a fellow human being. And, even though she has been through some terribly difficult times with her own children, she has a heart for people whose kids are sick—even for something as relatively minor as an appendix operation or a broken arm. She realizes that when a child has to have surgery, the parents hurt over it.

Mom worried that my sister Ruth was going to be adversely affected by all those trips to the hospital. Ruth was sixteen months old when I was born—as healthy and happy as a little girl could be—then all at once her life became a series of visits to the hospital to see me, then later Josh and Sam. Mom wondered what would happen to Ruth's memories and emotions.

To this day, Ruth has never said anything negative or shown any adverse effects from spending all that time in the hospital with us. In fact, maybe it affected her positively—she went on to become a registered nurse!

In a way, you could almost say Ruth was treated unfairly. She was healthy and average-sized, so she never got out of any housework like we did. I remember a few times—very, very few—when Ruth complained she always had to do the dishes or whatever. Mom and Dad would try to get us boys to help out, but it wasn't always possible. I am frankly amazed Ruth didn't get bitter. I'm not saying she was perfect, but she handled that kind of unbalanced life so much better and with so much more grace than we had a right to expect. She's incredible.

The time I spent in the hospital was a shaping force in making me the person I am today. I don't know how much good my time there did me physically, but I know that mentally and spiritually, I am a much stronger person for it. In the hospital my mind became sharper and more analytical. I learned to use my mind to keep me occupied, and that is a big win to a kid who is confined to a hospital room for months on end.

BEING TYPICAL IN AN ATYPICAL SITUATION

lickety-click…Clickety-click…Clickety-click…

My mother still remembers the rhythmic clicking sound it made when I, as a toddler in leg casts, clicked my heels together. It made not only the memorable noise, but also a little pile of cast dust beneath my feet.

I can remember how confined and fidgety I'd feel when I was in those body casts. There was a metal bar between the ankles that spread the legs out wide, which made it awkward to move around or do the simplest things. If you've ever had your arm or leg or even your foot in a cast, you know how terribly uncomfortable they can be. You can't move, and it's only a matter of time before you have an itch you desperately want to scratch.

Now think about the term "body cast." Your whole body—from your toes to the top of your chest—in a cast. There are only a few strategic gaps in the cast, but they aren't perfectly engineered for leaning back against a slippery toilet seat. Imagine the confinement you'd feel or the discomfort of that itch that is almost always there. One good thing came from those body cast periods, though: I sure developed upper body strength dragging all that weight across the floor.

When you are in a body cast, the only thing you really want is to have some independence. That's precisely what I wanted when I was a kid: simple normalcy. I just wanted to be a typical kid who went out and played with his friends, went to school, got in arguments with his brothers (I did that anyway), and all the other things kids do.

But life in the Roloff home was anything but typical. Typical families just don't have two dwarf children and a third with a defective heart. I'm sure my parents would have wanted things to be more typical. They didn't choose the situation we were in. If you'd asked them before we were born what kind of physical condition they wanted their kids in, I'm sure they'd have answered, "Tall and healthy."

No parents in their right minds would choose to have three disabled kids. They'd want healthy kids who could go out and do the same things other kids could do. Most of all, they'd want their kids to be accepted. Not rejected. Not left behind by the other kids. They'd want them to make friends and not be lonely.

For reasons we have no way of understanding, my parents were assigned the task of caring for three disabled kids. That gave them some serious life choices. How would they respond? They chose not to get bitter or angry about our situation, no matter how difficult it was. They chose to love us and care for us the best they could. They also chose to make our lives as normal as possible.

Even when everyone was home from the hospital, there was always evidence that sick kids lived there. There were Sam and me in our body casts and Josh breathing from an oxygen tank. In that respect, ours was not the typical family. But there were those things that let us and everyone else know that the Roloffs were, despite everything, still a regular family.

LIFE GOES ON

My parents, though they were present for every medical procedure we had, can't remember who had which surgery or what medication we took. They're not trying to repress bad memories, it's just that they believed we didn't need to live all the time in what Mom calls "the hospital mentality." It was the survival mode, and we saw it during the times my brothers or I were in the hospital.

When you look at some of the things my family went through when I was a child, it might be easy to forget that outside the stays in the hospital, the surgeries, the therapies, and the pain, we still had to do the typical day-to-day things families do. Things such as Dad earning a living for us and Mom doing the mountains of laundry four kids generate, taking kids to and from school, attending church, and enjoying family time. My parents weren't about to let handicaps stop their family from enjoying an all-American life.

Had we all been healthy, things probably would have been different financially for our family. But it was very expensive taking care of three disabled kids. Just the expense of the trips back and forth to the hospital was a financial strain, and we weren't left with a lot of extra income. I'm sure it was a struggle to get by, but as far as we kids knew, we were never in need of anything. To us, it seemed like a normal life; we just never knew anything different.

Early on, Dad worked as a carpenter, then later as a truck driver. He was always able to make a living for us. Later, he and Mom made some extra money buying old houses, cleaning them up, painting them, and selling them for a profit. Mom and Dad had a knack for making the proverbial silk purse out of a sow's ear when it came to fixing up old houses. They could take the filthiest, nastiest-looking house around and, with a little elbow grease and paint, turn it into something anyone would be happy to call home.

Dad was a work machine. He'd put in his time behind the wheel of his truck, then he'd come home, put on his carpenter's belt with its huge twenty-ounce framing hammer, and go to work on some project around the house. There were times when he worked ninety hours a week to keep the bills paid, provide for our needs, and sometimes give us just a little more.

That, in turn, made the days tougher for Mom, since she was left to take care of things at home. I'm not talking about the basic, everyday running of a household, either. I'm talking about everything that was such a part of our family, like taking us to and from doctor's appointments, carting us around when we couldn't walk because we were in body casts, and spending as much time as she could visiting us when we were in the hospital.

Just getting us around was a major undertaking. It was incredible how many ways Dad thought of for us to get about. Dad and Mom couldn't always carry us, so they had to think of ways to make it so we could go out in public, especially when we got too big to be pushed around in a stroller.

Dad made carts to wheel us around, some of which were downright ingenious. It amazes me to think about what can be done with a piece of plywood, some strapping, and four caster wheels.

FAMILY TIME

Dad and Mom set an example for me that I try to follow with my own kids: doing things with my kids and being there for them. Even in the midst of the chaos that often was our life, Dad and Mom made sure we spent family time together.

I'm sure it's difficult for someone who hasn't been confined or institutionalized for months on end to understand the way I longed for things most people take for granted. After spending three months at a time in the hospital, just the feeling of getting out and breathing fresh air—as opposed to that antiseptic-smelling hospital air—or riding around in the car with the family was incredible to me.

My parents made getting out of the hospital an exciting time for me and my brothers. They always had something for us to do when we got out. Spending time outdoors was a big part of our family life, and we spent a lot of time in the mountains. Dad loved to take the family camping or hiking.

For several years we lived only a few hours' drive from Yosemite National Park in California. We went often. If you've ever been to Yosemite, you know what I'm saying (and feeling) when I tell you how awesome that place is. The huge cliffs and raging waterfalls are spectacular.

Back then I had a favorite attraction: the fire-fall. Every evening the park rangers used to build this huge fire at the top of Glacier Point. Just after dark they'd sweep the glowing coals over the sheer drop. For ten minutes the flaming embers would put on a spectacular show for the campers on the valley floor.

Dad was great at inventing ways of toting Sam and me around on our hikes. He'd wrap us in plastic garbage bags and duct tape (to keep our body casts from getting wet), throw us over his shoulder, and carry us over some serious white water. I was always scared to death. If he'd ever slipped it would've been tragic. But he never did.

I remember many times when we'd be driving along through a wilderness area and Dad would see a challenging cliff or huge boulder. He'd stop the car and scamper up the side of that cliff like a mountain goat. Then he'd come back down and tell us, "I can get you boys up there." We'd say, "No, Dad, please! We're fine right here." But he'd insist. So he'd throw us over his shoulders and up we'd go. It was terrifying—but always worth it.

I don't know if it was his Marine training or what, but in all the years Dad carried us around, he never dropped us, even in the most treacherous conditions.

We also would go to Christian family camps in a spot in the Santa Cruz Mountains in California. It was in a fairly rugged area with some great trails. There were always things to do, both for the kids and for the adults.

Being a little person on a hike with average-sized high schoolers was a difficult thing. I couldn't keep up! I couldn't do all the things at camp that I would liked to have done, simply because of my physical limitations. It was an awkward time for me. But it was also a great time because it stretched me as a person, and it allowed me to see the compassion of the other kids, who did all they could to help me keep up. I learned things during those summers that would help me, years later, when I became the father of a little person.

HITTING THE ROAD

One day, not long after a release from the hospital, Dad came home with some exciting news: "I've got three weeks of vacation," he told Mom. "I can take three weeks at once or three one-week vacations. What do you want to do?"

"Well, we've always wanted to make a cross-country trip," Mom said. "This might be the time."

It was true that we'd all talked about a cross-country drive. Dad had told Sam and me when we were in the hospital that we would be taking the trip sometime after we got out. We wanted to see how many of the forty-eight continental U.S. states we could visit, and how many states' stickers we could collect to put on the family van. Now it seemed like the time was right.

We had three weeks to prepare until Dad got his vacation. We planned our route, making sure we could stop and visit family along the way. Mom made matching flowered bell-bottom outfits for all of the kids (it *was* the sixties), just in case we got separated from the pack.

We had a 1969 Volkswagen bus Dad had altered to accommodate a married couple and their four kids—including two boys who couldn't sit down in the seats. Dad solved that problem by rigging up the interior of the van so Sam and I could ride comfortably in our body casts. He set up a rack that would hold us in place so that we hung in the van like a couple swinging sides of beef. It must have been a strange sight: two kids in body casts hanging in the van like that, but it was the most comfortable, practical, and safe way Dad could think of to do it.

Finally, the day came to start our trip. We got in the van and headed out from Concord, California, to New York City. We traveled in the van, talked in the van, ate our meals in the van, and slept in the van. We would drive all day—stopping to see relatives or sights along the way—then stop at a truck stop to eat dinner. The rest of us would go to sleep and Dad would keep driving. We'd go to sleep in one state and wake up in another. I think Dad's years as a truck driver had him well conditioned for that kind of driving. Even so, I still don't know how he did it.

How did six people live comfortably in a Volkswagen van? I have to give my parents the credit for that. They used our time, our money, and all our other resources efficiently. Being a truck driver, Dad was good at fitting things in small spaces. Every space in and on that van—under and behind the seats, in the luggage compartments, on the luggage racks—was in use for storage.

Sleeping arrangements were a little cramped but still comfortable. Josh and I slept in the back section of the van in hammocks; Ruth had a hammock that could be unhooked and folded; Mom and Dad had a mattress that went from the backseat of the van to the front and folded up during the day; and Sam, who was only two at the time, had a piece of foam between the front seats.

We didn't stop to eat in the finest restaurants, but we didn't starve, either. We were on a pretty tight budget on this trip, and that budget didn't leave room for a lot of extras. Mom made the food money stretch when we were on the road, using the camp stove and some old-fashioned homemade victuals, including plenty of granola she had made and stored in Tupperware containers. The granola became a staple for us for breakfast and for snacks—to this day, I won't touch the stuff!

We didn't make it to all forty-eight states. I think we came up about ten states short. What we did get, though, were some great memories. We spent this fantastic time together, just a "normal" family summer vacation.

ONE STEP FORWARD, TWO STEPS BACK

That vacation was the beginning of the farm bug in my Dad and I guess in me as well. We'd passed all these fantastic farms and ranches during our drive. Each time we did, I could hear Dad oohing and aahing in the front seat.

It wasn't long after we got back that Dad started taking Sunday drives into the countryside just north of San Francisco. He found (and later bought) this great little one and a half acre ranchette up in the Santa Rosa foothills. It had a brand-new ranch-style house that was a step up from anything we'd had in the past. Just across the pasture was a creek and a large wooded area for us to explore and play in.

I had just finished a major operation and was still receiving physical therapy to get my leg strength back. I remember watching the phone man climb the telephone pole in our backyard to hook up our phone. After he left, I told Josh and Sam I was going to climb that pole.

I climbed up on Dad's wheelbarrow and stood up on the several concrete bags inside. As I tried to reach the lower peg on that pole, the wheelbarrow flipped over, caught my leg, and *Wham!* I'd been out of the body cast less than a month and here I was, flat on my back, screaming, "I broke my leg!"

Back into a cast.

Breaking my leg didn't cause us to move back to the city, but I think what happened the following year did. We had this well-stocked lake up the road from us. One day we were out fishing when Mom came running up with a frantic look on her face. She had been cooking some doughnuts when the grease caught fire and ignited the entire kitchen. She called the fire department, but by the time they got there the kitchen had been totaled, and the rest of the house was ruined by the smoke. We had to live at friends' and relatives' homes for several weeks while the house was repaired. She later told us how she panicked after the fire broke out, running around the house thinking we might still be trapped with our body casts somewhere. Of course we were safe up at the fishing hole.

I think that fire caused Mom to sort of lose interest in living so far out in the country because we moved back to the city shortly after that.

INSTILLING PROPER ATTITUDES

My parents would never have allowed me or my brothers to take a "poor me" attitude. They didn't allow themselves to wallow in self-pity, and they wouldn't allow us that luxury, either.

They were great about teaching my brothers and me to have a good attitude, even when we were in pain or emotionally down. They taught us to be humble (my mother still seems to believe it is her calling to keep me from becoming arrogant), to be courteous, and, most of all, not to be obnoxious and demanding simply because we were disabled. I can remember both of them telling me, "Don't be a spoiled handicapped brat." I didn't fully understand what they meant at the time, but I do now. My parents simply wanted us to understand that our disabilities were no excuse for us to be bossy, demanding, or rude.

I remember one incident that showed me how far my parents were willing to go to teach me to have proper attitudes. I was about twelve years old, and I was shooting my BB gun at a transformer, one of those big canister-looking things atop telephone poles. I liked the sound the BB made when it hit, and I was having a good time. One of the shots ricocheted off the canister and went through the window of a dentist's office that was next to our house. The BB broke the glass and nearly hit the receptionist in the face. The front door of the office flew open, and a man I later found out was the receptionist's boyfriend came storming out after me.

I ran home as fast as my crutches would take me and stood next to my mother, who was watering the flower bed at the time. The man came in my direction, enraged and ready to exact some retribution—or at least to throw a little scare into me. My mother stepped between me and the man and asked what had happened. When he explained to her what he was angry about and that no one was hurt, she said, "I'll take care of this."

Mom turned to me and said, "Matthew, come inside." At that point, all Mom planned to do was give me a talking to, take away the gun for a while, and that would be the end of it. But I made the situation worse with an attitude that said, "It's no big deal!" That was a mistake.

My mother had never liked that BB gun. She didn't like it when I had first gotten it, which was when we lived in the country. She was always worried about me shooting out my eye like a friend of mine had done a few years before. Now she liked the gun even less because we were living in the city. She wanted that gun gone, and now she had a good excuse to make it disappear.

"Matt, where is the gun?" she asked, and I told her where I'd hidden it. "Go get it!"

I handed it over to my mother, who had gotten something of her own while I was gone: a ten-pound sledge hammer. My mother, this sweet, loving woman from whom I had seen nothing but compassion and tenderness my whole life, had turned into a different person.

With the hammer in her hand and the BB gun in her sights, she flew into a rage the likes of which I had never before seen. Mom carried the gun to the sidewalk, laid it down, and, with unbridled fury, lit into it with the hammer. Each time she brought the hammer down, she seemed to enjoy it more. She pounded the gun until it was nothing but a pile of broken, twisted plastic and metal, until there was little left of it that even faintly resembled part of a gun.

I went into a fit of my own at that moment. Mom hadn't made a secret of her dislike for my gun, but I liked it. I liked shooting my gun, and I'd become pretty good at it, too. It had become one of my favorite toys, and now my own mother had made sure I'd never have a chance to play with it again. To me, every blow of the hammer was like a blow against me personally. While Mother poured out her anger on my gun, I poured out my anger on her, tearfully letting her know that I thought she was the meanest person in the world.

I was so angry I stormed off, got on my bike, and ran away from home, resolving never to return. I stayed gone, too, visiting friends and wandering the streets till well past dark that night. My parents had called Eric, my best friend, to see if he knew where I was. At first Eric said he hadn't seen me, but later he admitted I'd told him I was going to sleep at a Catholic church that night and that I was never going home.

After talking to Eric for a while, Mom and Dad got a general idea where I might be, so they jumped in the Volkswagen van and headed out into the night to look for me. Finally, they spotted me. They pulled up next to me, and Dad called out, "Hey, Matt!" I swerved away from them on my bike and ducked down an alley. My father jumped out of the van and took off after me on foot. He finally overtook me, picked me up, and carried me to the van. He put me—kicking and screaming—in the van and held me there while Mom, crying her eyes out, drove us home.

They put me to bed, and I cried myself to sleep. By the next morning things seemed to have blown over. All was a little quiet in the Roloff home that morning, but there didn't seem to be a lot of anger spilling out.

Ironically, that was the day I was scheduled to give the a speech for the Optimists' Club community. I had been chosen to speak about how you can overcome adversity. I was going to talk about how I was actually glad that I had my disability, and how it made me so much stronger. I wasn't feeling especially optimistic at the moment, though.

That was one of those terrible episodes that can happen in even the most loving families. But during it all, there was one thing Mom and Dad made clear to me: No matter how angry I got at them, no matter how upset they were at me, no matter what the nature of our disagreements were, they weren't going to let me spend the night wandering the streets. Nor were they going to allow me to cop a "so-what" attitude when I'd messed up.

DEALING WITH PEOPLE

Despite the pain, the isolation, and the discomfort my condition brought on me, somehow I always knew things would eventually get better for me. I knew the pain would pass, that I would get discharged from the hospital, and that I would be out and about with my family and friends. And because of my mother and father's training and discipline, I knew how to treat people—and have them treat me—in an acceptable way.

I learned not to expect pity or a special break because I was disabled, and

I learned to accept it when it came. But my parents also taught all of us how to respond when someone said something about our condition—either out of pity or ridicule. When that happened, it was nothing more to my parents than an opportunity to teach another lesson about life.

Dad and Mom seemed to know how to respond to my brother and me when we were hurt over something someone said or did concerning our short stature. Dad, true to his nature, would speak up and confront an adult who said something demeaning to one of us. But when it came to the kids we knew, our parents taught us how to respond without going to blows. They never encouraged us to smart off or to become belligerent when one of our classmates teased us.

I remember coming home from school one day, upset because someone had called me, of all things, "short." I walked in the house and said, "Dad, someone called me short."

His response was to look at me incredulously and say, "Well, aren't you?"

"Well, yeah, I am."

"Then what's the problem?"

I didn't have an answer for that. Yes, I was short—much shorter than my classmates. At that point, it sunk in that what my classmate had done was just state the obvious. Dad was always very straightforward about that sort of thing. Dad would say, "If anyone ever tells you you're small, just tell 'em they have a great pair of eyeballs."

My parents were at the receiving end of more than their share of unkind remarks themselves. I can remember Mom getting chastised by people when they'd see her carrying Josh while Sam and I were walking along on our crutches. Josh would be turning purple and struggling just to get enough oxygen to keep himself conscious, but people would challenge Mom: "How can you carry that healthy boy when you have these two boys on crutches?"

There was a lot of wisdom in the things Mom and Dad taught us when we were kids. Instead of focusing on what we couldn't do, they encouraged us to look for and develop the gifts we did have.

MY STRUGGLES AND VICTORIES IN SCHOOL

In most ways I was a typical kid. I went to school, made friends, and played outside. We used to play hide-and-seek on those long California evenings, using the streetlight as base. Since I couldn't run up and down the block as fast as the other kids, I learned to be creative about hiding closer to the base, maybe in a space too small to suspect.

Like anybody else, I had conflicts with my parents, I got in arguments with my brothers and sister, and I even got in fights with other kids at school. I had days of typical teenage depression, and I had crushes on girls, and I had teachers I considered my "favorites."

Mom and Dad sent me to private Christian schools for a time, and when I was in a body cast and needed special attention I went to *El Portel Del Norte,* a Bay Area school for disabled students. But mostly I attended public schools in the San Francisco Bay area.

I'm not proud to admit this, but I wasn't the best student I could have been. I wasn't bad. I got decent grades all the way through school. I got the grades I needed to get. If I needed a B average to be eligible for sports or to get a lower rate on my car insurance, I got it. If I needed to ace a certain test to make that average, I got an A on that test. And in the subjects I really liked—auto shop, for example—I got good grades simply because I enjoyed being in the class. But there was an underlying feeling on my parents'—and my teachers'—part that I could have done much better than I did.

I know my time in hospitals put me behind the curve when it came to my education. I had to take third grade twice. As time went on, I missed more and more school because I was in the hospital, and the discomfort I felt often made it difficult, if not impossible, to study. Shriners had a system in which tutors came in to teach us a couple of hours a day, but that didn't make up for the six hours in school we missed every day we were in there.

Largely because of these factors, by the time I got to high school, I didn't know *how* to study. I was an intelligent teenager, but not good when it came to sitting down and plowing through a stack of homework.

I remember something that happened to me about the second or third day of my freshman year in high school. Everything was new to me. I was just starting to figure out how to get from one class to another. My math teacher called on me to answer a very basic math problem. It wasn't two plus two, but it was something a freshman in high school should know. I drew a blank. I remember sitting there, feeling like I was going to cry because I felt so stupid.

A day or so after that I was still trying to figure out how I should respond. It was a critical crossroads for me: should I just curl up and die, laugh it off with the class, or come up with some other creative solution to rebuild my demolished ego? Just then I saw a poster urging people to run for class office. *That's it!* I thought. *Not only will that put me in the middle of the action, it will also show them I'm not as dumb as I look.*

I remember wondering what would happen if I ran but didn't win. Would I be resilient enough to recover from such a double blow so early in my high school career? Probably. I just knew I couldn't lose.

I launched an aggressive and active campaign. The night before the election I had several friends climb onto the roof of the school and hang a gigantic sign made from several bedsheets sewn together with the words, "VOTE ROLOFF CLASS PRESIDENT" printed on it. After a sweet, well-earned victory, I spent the rest of that year more focused on fund-raisers and class events than on study. Once again, I thought I had a good excuse for not studying.

I wasn't a total goof-off in school. I was motivated to do the things I enjoyed. In high school I wrestled, took auto mechanics and wood shop, snow skied, and spent lots of time with my friends. I was well liked in the community. I even won several speech contests.

But I would do anything it took to get out of the more traditional schoolwork. I worked harder at getting around schoolwork than I would have if I'd just done it.

As most parents in this situation would be, mine were frustrated at what they considered my mediocrity in school. They knew I was capable of more, even though my grades were still above average. Dad didn't attend my high school graduation. I had completed all the necessary courses, but Dad didn't think I deserved to graduate because I hadn't applied myself. To his way of thinking, a high school graduation ceremony should be a celebration of achievement, and I'd done nothing more than what I had to in order to get by. Now he says he regrets not going, but looking back on it, I know he was right.

Mom never saw me as average. She knew I had talent and ability, that I wouldn't be just another kid. Even in kindergarten, she saw that in me, and she pleaded with my teacher to push me to accomplish more. "Well," the teacher told her, "Matt's never going to set the world on fire. He's just an average child." Mom was so angry she could barely speak, but she managed to keep her composure and let the teacher know that anyone could see I wasn't average.

My parents wanted me to go to college, and I did for a very short time— although I still don't have a college credit to my name. I quickly found out college wasn't for me. I started taking some classes at a community college, but I floundered badly. I didn't have the kind of self-discipline it took to succeed in college, and I didn't stay long. My decision not to pursue a college education also didn't set well with Mom and Dad. They were, to put it mildly, disappointed.

I've done very well in my line of work, but sometimes I wonder what I could have accomplished had I been a better student. I have a hunch I would have done better, and I know I would have been better at writing and math. I regret now that I didn't put more effort into my schoolwork, and I work hard to encourage and motivate my kids to do well in school. I want them to take pride in giving whatever they do their best effort, and that includes schoolwork.

CROSSING BARRIERS

While I didn't get great grades in school, if there had been a grading system for socializing, I would have gotten an easy A.

I was never shy around people. I learned early how to compensate for my disabilities by developing confidence approaching people. I've always been able to mix well with people from different social, ethnic, or economic groups. I've always believed that people are people, and it doesn't matter to me what side of the tracks they live on, what color their skin is, or how much money they make. I had lots of friends in school.

We all remember the different social cliques in high school: the book-worms, the jocks, the stoners, and the rest. I was the kind of kid who liked to spend time with kids from all the groups. I was friendly to everybody. Sure, I had my own group of friends, and I spent the lion's share of my time with them. For example, I wrestled in high school, so I had quite a few friends who wrestled. I didn't do drugs or smoke, but I liked some of the people who did, and I would spend time with them. I talked to kids the others saw as outcasts.

One of my friends in high school was a big, tough kid whom I'll call Jimmy. Jimmy was not only our heavyweight wrestler, he also had a black belt in judo. He was without question the toughest kid I knew. He didn't look that tough. He wasn't very tall, and he was built a little like a sumo wrestler. But I saw quite a number of much bigger guys take a beating from Jimmy.

Jimmy could be a genuinely nice guy, but he came from a broken home. His mother did the best she could to keep him out of trouble. She'd say, "Matt, keep an eye on Jimmy. Sometimes he just doesn't know which way to go." But sometimes trouble had a way of finding him. Jimmy had a heart of gold, and he was a good friend. He took it upon himself to look out for his little buddy.

I once had a problem with another kid, but it wasn't a big deal. We were teasing one another, and things went a little too far. We both laughed about it, and I thought that was the end of it. But when Jimmy heard about this little nonincident from a mutual friend, he "took care of" the kid.

"I found out what happened to you the other day, and I took care of the kid for you," Jimmy proudly told me.

"You took care of him?" I asked. "What do you mean?"

Jimmy explained that he had pushed the kid around, then deposited him in the nearest trash receptacle.

"Jimmy! We were just joking around!" I told him. "Don't go beating on people for me like that."

Jimmy helped me out of a tight spot once. I must have been around twelve or thirteen years old when I finally managed to talk my folks into buying me a skateboard. I'm sure their short-lived hesitation was caused by both the dangers of skateboarding and the practical fact that I would probably never use it. Buying a skateboard would be a wasted investment on our already tight budget. How would a guy like me use a skateboard anyway?

I learned to balance myself on that tiny plank and push myself with my crutches. This was about the same time I was starting to explore farther and farther from the house. I rode that board everywhere around town.

We had a street nearby with lots of shops. A few friends from junior high told me about a gaming room upstairs in one of the shops. It was, in fact, a pool hall. I knew my mom wouldn't want me up there. But the temptation to see what it looked like was too great.

I pulled up to the back door and left my yellow banana skateboard at the bottom of the long staircase. I went up. It was a pool hall, all right. Lots of real tough-looking kids. I wasn't afraid of them because I knew Jimmy knew them all. I quickly toured the place, trying to act like I belonged, but I didn't see Jimmy. I hurried back down the stairs, feeling quite proud of myself for my risky behavior. I was only five steps from my quick getaway when I got that sickening feeling you get when something valuable isn't where you left it. It hit hard. I was only up there five minutes and *somebody took my board!*

I had to walk the eight blocks home, feeling something between stupid and scared. What would I tell my folks? I could barely sleep that night. I couldn't wait to get to school the next day to track Jimmy down and see if he could somehow help me out.

"Jimmy, my skateboard got ripped off," I said. "I went to the pool hall for a minute. When I came out, it was gone."

"No problem," Jimmy said. "I'll get you another one. What color do you want?"

"No, Jimmy!" I said. "I don't want you to take somebody else's skateboard. I want *my* skateboard. I want you to try to track mine down."

Living in the metro area of San Francisco, I knew my chances of getting the board back were pretty slim. But Jimmy was well connected, and he put the word out that my board had been stolen. Sure enough, Jimmy showed up two days later with my skateboard. I was glad not to know how Jimmy got it or who had taken it. I was just happy to get my skateboard back.

LOOKING OUT FOR MYSELF

As I got older, Dad gave me some half-joking advice when it came to kids who bothered me at school. He'd tell me, "Well, you know how to use your crutches."

I very seldom felt the need to whack someone across the shins with my sticks, but I do remember reacting violently one time to a kid who was bothering me in gym class. I was in a wheelchair at the time, and one day I was dribbling a basketball. The kid came up behind me and started pushing me around in the chair. This was not the first thing this particular kid had done to irritate me. I asked him to stop, but he laughed and kept it up. Finally, when I had a shot at him, I threw the basketball in his face and bloodied his nose. He never bothered me again.

I went through a spell in which I was quite the hothead. I had an attitude that even though I was little, I wasn't going to take guff off anybody. I'd let people who bothered me know that I had no limits, "no ceiling" to what I would do. I loved giving tough guys the impression I had something up my sleeve when I got in a confrontation.

Whenever my buddies and I would drive around, I would sit in my car and keep my arms down so guys wouldn't see my short arms. My big tall buddies would cower down in the back seat, not wanting to get in a fight because of my antagonism. I never wanted to fight anyone either, but I was not in the least bit afraid to get in people's faces if I felt they were doing something inappropriate or belligerent.

It got to be a game for me, to see how close I could get to a physical confrontation and still talk my way out of it. I was good at it, too. I had a way of egging on the situation, then using my sense of humor—and my appearance—

to disarm it. I would hide my dwarfism the best I could until the point where it was absolutely going to go to blows, then I would reveal my size, point my crutch at the guy's face, and let him know in no uncertain terms that I had full confidence in my physical ability to take him down. Even my friends watching from the car would later tell me, "You were very convincing, Matt. We even thought you could take him, just from your confidence." More often than not, the other guy and I would end up laughing about our confrontation.

One of my most memorable episodes took place at a Bay Area 7-11 store. I was driving around with a couple of my friends, and we decided to stop off to get some sodas. I pulled into the parking lot, then waited outside as my friends went inside to make our purchases. I didn't even notice the car pull up next to me in the parking lot. I was just sitting there, staring off into space in the general direction of the driver of the car that pulled up. It was a nice day, so I had my windows down, and I just sat there thinking about who knows what.

"What are you staring at?" the driver said.

I wasn't staring at anything. But I couldn't resist. I was like a fisherman who gets a bite on the line. When you get a bite, you yank. "I'm staring at *you*," I said.

I'm sure this guy saw me sitting in the front seat of my car and thought I was just some short smart aleck that needed a beating. I had my arms down, so he couldn't tell there was anything different about me. He said, "You little punk, I'm gonna teach you a lesson."

This guy was on my hook. He was mine. I fixed my glare at him, and, in the most stern tone I could muster I said, "If I have to get out of this car, you're gonna be sorry."

No way was this guy going to pass on a challenge like that. He opened the car door and jumped to his feet. I followed suit. As far as he knew, we were about to go off on each another. He was ready to rumble. I got out of my car, grabbed my crutches, and charged from behind my car. His eyes went as big as silver dollars.

I knew I had him. He wanted out. I could see it in his eyes. Beating up a dwarf on crutches doesn't score you any tough guy points. He was searching for an escape. He instantly threw his hands up as if he were surrendering. "You're right! You're right! I'm sorry!" he said, walking away from me.

"You're lucky," I called out after him, trying to choke back the laughter. "I'm going to let you go this time. Next time, watch yourself!"

I'm glad to report now that I've outgrown that sort of behavior. I realized it wasn't a good idea to look for confrontations, even though I knew the vast majority of guys would never fight me. I'm also grateful to report that, despite myself, I never got hurt doing that kind of thing. I know now I could have been hurt, or worse, if I'd messed with the wrong people. These days, people get shot over small arguments.

I was starting to get an aggressive personality when I was in school. Fortunately I found a constructive outlet. It was an outlet that gave me wonderful memories of my time as a high school athlete.

SUCCESS WITH WRESTLING

It surprises people to hear it, but sports and athletics can be a big part of a little person's life. I'm not talking about as a spectator, but as a participant. Of course, there are limitations to what I could have done as an athlete, but I was able to find my niche in high school sports.

I was involved in numerous athletic activities for handicapped students, including what would become an annual wheelchair football game for the area's high schools. There were several teams in the Bay Area, one for about every three high schools. We played on tennis courts or in gymnasiums, using a Nerf football and flags so that the defense could "down" the ball. We made it a big event, too, inviting disc jockeys from area radio stations to serve as masters of ceremonies and to play music for us.

I was also into downhill snow skiing, and I became pretty good at it, too. I was fluid and fast on the skis, and kind of fearless when it came to flying down the slopes. I started skiing when I was in junior high school when my parents took us skiing for the first time. I was hooked, and I went on to compete in several events for disabled people.

Then there was the sport I competed in on a high school varsity level: wrestling. Wrestling is a great sport for a little guy, even for someone like me. In wrestling you compete only with kids your size because you compete according to weight classifications. No one had to make any allowances or adjustments for me when I wrestled, either. I went out and competed against guys my weight, just like everybody else.

I wrestled all four years for Crestmore High School in San Francisco, which was a Bay Area wrestling dynasty in the late seventies. I did pretty well all four years. I wasn't great, but I had a winning record, won my district a couple of years, then did well in regionals. I was never pinned. I got a lot of byes because I wrestled at the ninety-five-pound division, and there weren't a lot of wrestlers that size. Even in the matches I actually got to wrestle, I won more than I lost.

I had an advantage over some wrestlers at my weight because I'd built up great upper body strength from walking around on crutches. I also had a very low center of gravity, and my short legs made it almost impossible for someone to take me down. I'd go out on the mat, shake hands, drop to my knees and shoot for the legs. Sometimes my opponents would circle around me and take me down from behind, but I had a knack for getting escapes and reversals because of my upper body strength.

By the time I was a senior, most of the coaches in our district knew my moves and tricks. The opposing coaches had a great strategy against me. They'd instruct their wrestlers to circle around me when I went to my knees, get the two-point takedown, then let me up before I had a chance to get a reversal. That was smart coaching, looking back on it, because it was two points for one every time someone took me down then gave up an escape.

Wrestling gave me some great memories, the most vivid being a match I wrestled in my junior year against Tony Bagnoral, a fellow little person. Tony, who is still a friend of mine, wrestled one weight class up from me at Arogan High School. Even though he outweighed me by five pounds—and when you weigh less than a hundred pounds, five pounds really makes a difference—my coaches and teammates wanted me to wrestle him. I wanted to wrestle him myself. At the time, I didn't worry that anyone might see the match as some kind of sideshow. I just wanted to see how I would do against another little person.

I wasn't a better wrestler than Tony. He was bigger and more agile than I was. Still, it was a great match. He had me down most of the first round. He was getting the best of me, but somehow I got a reversal on him late in the round and pinned him. I still remember how the crowd went wild at the Crestmore High School gymnasium when the referee slapped the mat to give me the fall. I remember, too, how people at school talked all that week about the match between the Bay Area's two little person wrestlers.

That match is still an outstanding memory among a lot of great memories I have from my days in school. Those were the years when I eased my way into the "real world," the days when I learned to adjust to life outside the relative security of the Roloff home. They were fun days, challenging days, and memorable days. They were the days when I started to realize that, even as a little person, I was going to make it.

GETTING MY START IN THE WORLD OF WORK

My father told me something as I began my work life as a teenager that became invaluable to me: "Matt, you're going to have to learn to use your mind to make it. You won't be working at McDonald's like the rest of your friends."

Dad was right. It was obvious from the beginning I couldn't do some of the most basic tasks required of a young guy when he first enters the world of work. For example, I'd have a tough time working at a fast-food joint because I was too short to work the grills or see over the countertops. I couldn't work at a grocery store because I couldn't reach the upper shelves (I still have to ask for help with that when I go shopping with my wife).

I obviously had physical limitations that would keep me from doing certain tasks. Mom and Dad knew that, and I came to appreciate their sense of realism when they talked to me and my brothers about what we would be able to do. They taught us not to allow our disabilities to keep us from enjoying successful lives, but they weren't about to baby-talk us or make us cultivate unrealistic dreams or goals. Mom and Dad taught us there were things we would have talents and skills in, and we could be successful if we pursued careers that used them.

I have huge physical limitations, but I have more than made up for them with the development of my mind and personality. All the things I've gone through because of my physical condition worked to mold me into a person with the confidence to accomplish what I set out to accomplish, even when it means counting on the help of others to do it.

THE INSTIGATOR

Mom likes to tell people how before my third birthday I was the most darling, compliant child any parent could have hoped for. I had kind of an innocent look about me when I was very young. In fact, I was the poster child for one of the East-West Shrine football games in California. The poster had a photograph of me sitting in a crib, with a "Won't you help?" look on my face.

Later on, though, something changed. I didn't become a troublemaker—I didn't give my parents, my teachers, or the staff at the hospital any major problems. But I developed an edge, a certain something that gave me the ability to get things going, to influence people. I've always had an energetic personality. I always like to be doing something, and people respond well to that. I'm also a maverick in my methods, and I'm never short of ideas for things to do.

I know this part of my personality comes from being little. It's a way of compensating for lack of physical stature. I know that if I were shy and looked the way I do, I would have spent a lot of time sitting in a corner. But something inside me let me know early that I needed to overcome any natural tendency to shrink away from people. I knew I had to be a stronger, more outgoing person if I were going to thrive in this world.

I was a leader of the pack when I was in the hospital. I could always get the other kids to cooperate with me. If there was something we wanted to do, I was able to organize the kids so we could do it. I pushed the nurses just far enough to get something without getting myself or my friends in trouble.

I was also the kid who couldn't pass on a dare.

Someone dared a group of us to break out of the hospital and wheel ourselves down to the local store a few blocks away. I was in a body cast at the time, but I couldn't pass on a dare like that. We'd already taken some heat from wheelchair races down the halls, but I still wanted to take my friends up on this dare. With a little inside help (I won't give that secret away) we got the key to the back door and broke out. We made it to the store and back, but not before one of the nurses discovered we had escaped.

The hospital administration was none too pleased that we'd gotten out. On the record, I was told if I pulled something like that again I would be in major trouble. Off the record, one of the nurses told my mom it was good to see us behaving like normal kids.

Not everything I did in the hospital had a mischievous edge to it. I learned that sometimes it's best to work within the system to get what you and your friends want. During one hospital stay, my friends and I talked about how nice it would be to have a room where we could relax and play games together away from the hospital rooms or halls. I wrote a letter to the hospital administration, suggesting that they clear out a room for the older kids to use for recreation. The administrators agreed, and not long after that we opened the "Teen Room," which was a lounge where we played chess, board games and listened to music.

My motivation for the things I instigated at the hospital was never to make things rough on the nurses or the administration. I just liked making life in the hospital more interesting and more comfortable for me and my friends. When I thought of something to do, it only seemed natural to make it happen.

I had a way of making things happen at home, too. My mother always preferred to have her kids close to home so she could keep an eye on us and make sure everything was okay. My brothers and I were close, and we loved spending time together. Fortunately, the kids in our neighborhood would come over to play with us. We usually had a yard full of kids, and I could always think of things for us to do. We were always building forts, holding backyard carnivals, playing army games and hide-and-seek, and doing the other things kids do to have fun.

One summer, Dad built us a big playhouse. A beauty. It was about eight by sixteen feet, which is pretty big for a backyard playhouse. We had a great summer playing in that house. One of our activities was a bit of excavation under the house. I got the idea from watching *Hogan's Heroes* on TV. Little by little, we dug out under the floor of the house. One day, Mom walked around the back of the playhouse and saw that we had dug a six-foot-deep hole under the house. This scared her because she wondered if it were possible for the sides of the hole to cave in on us (actually, it probably was). Dad worried what could happen if the hole filled with water. It wasn't long before our great escape was thwarted.

AN ENTREPRENEURIAL SPIRIT

I don't come from what anyone would call an affluent background. Dad made enough for us to get by comfortably. To him, money was a tool to be used to take care of his family, and not a driving force in his life. I'm a lot like that now. I make a very comfortable living selling computer systems, but I'm not what you would consider rich.

Even though I have never cared about being rich, I've always been enterprising when it came to making an honest buck. I've never been afraid of a little hard work, even at an age when most kids don't even think about working. I almost always had something going to make money for myself. There was just something inside me that motivated me to work and make money.

When I was twelve, I surprised Mom and Dad by announcing I was going to get my first job. I told my mom, "I'm going to get a newspaper route," and asked her if she'd drive me to my appointment.

Mom agreed, even though (I found out later) she didn't think I had a chance of getting a route. Mom believed I was capable of handling it, but she didn't know how the distribution manager would react when he saw me, this kid who was a full head shorter than the smallest kid there that day.

I approached the distribution manager and talked to him for a while, telling him how enthusiastic I was to have a chance to work for him. I let him know how confident I was that I could do a good job for him, how I would be an asset for him. He believed me and gave me a great route that was only a few blocks from where we lived in San Francisco.

It was a twice-weekly paper, and my job was to deliver the paper and do the collections. Many times people would look at me and maybe they felt sorry for me, so they'd give me a nice tip. I didn't care why they gave me the tips, I just enjoyed the extra cash.

My brothers and I made money by holding Saturday backyard carnivals. We set up eight or nine stations, including little booths for bean bag throws, puppet shows, and different kinds of contests. I would lie awake at night for weeks beforehand planning out what each station would be and planning where we would get the materials to build them. The neighborhood kids would come spend their pennies, nickels, and dimes in our carnivals.

Before I could even drive, I started my own business: "Matt's Can Collecting Service." I collected recyclable aluminum cans by strategically setting out big barrels for people in industrial areas to put their cans. Then I would take them home to flatten them with my own little invention.

Using a little muscle and brain power, I designed a way to crush the cans flat so I could turn them in. A friend and I took a big slab of concrete we'd dragged to our backyard, drilled holes in it, put hooks in the holes, then rigged up a pulley system to lift the slab. When I raised it, my buddy would use a broom to sweep a pile of cans under the slab. I'd let go, and the slab would flatten the cans like pancakes. Then we'd turn in the cans to the recyclers and collect the money.

My brothers and I made something good out of a bad situation during the late seventies' gas shortages. As we watched drivers waiting impatiently in those long, slow-moving lines to buy gasoline, I remember thinking they'd probably like some refreshments. This was before the one-stop food/gas marts we have today. We asked the gas station owner if we could set up a table near his station and sell coffee and sodas to his customers-in-waiting. I convinced him that his customers would be much happier waiting in line if they had something to drink. He must've seen my point because he agreed to let us set up a table without taking any commission on our sales.

As a teenager, I made pretty good money working on cars. Although I don't really like doing it now, Dad thought I might have been a great auto mechanic. It seemed like I had a way with cars as a teenager. I took to working on them—particularly Volkswagens—quickly, and that led to a nice little business venture as a teenager.

There was a time when I had seven or eight different cars I was working on, all lined up in our driveway. Some of my projects were "basket cases" that needed complete engine overhauls. Others I just cleaned up, put a few chrome parts in the engine compartment, then sold them for a small profit. I'd buy Volkswagens that weren't running or were barely running or just needed a little tender loving care to make them drivable, do the work on them, then sell them for a profit. A few times, I made a thousand dollars on a car.

I was one of the auto mechanics class foremen, and I got a set of keys to the shop, so I always had access to tools to use on my cars. When I was sixteen, I bought an old Volkswagen and my best friend, Eric Jones, and I tore apart the engine, rebuilt it, and had it running. We sold the car for a profit. Another time I bought a car, then "donated" it to the shop class so the students could rebuild the engine. When they got it running, I sold it for a nice profit, too. My only concern was to put together a deal that worked for everybody. Finding and thinking up win-win deals would turn out to be one of my strongest assets.

ONE BIG BREAK

During my sophomore year in high school, I was invited to speak to the area Rotary Club. I spoke about what it was like to live life with a physical disability and how I believed I still had a good future, despite my physical problems. There must have been something in that speech that resonated because afterwards a man who became a key person in my life approached me. His name was Lou Carpine, and he was a bigwig with the Bay Area Sears stores. Lou said he was impressed with the speech and the attitude behind it. As he got ready to go, he handed me his card and said, "If you ever need anything, call me."

Although I was making money on my own, I had been thinking about looking for a regular job. I was a sophomore in high school at the time, and all my friends were getting jobs at fast-food restaurants, grocery stores, service stations, and other places teenagers typically work. One day, a few weeks after I had met Lou Carpine, I was talking to my mom about finding a job. We talked about what kinds of things I could and couldn't do because of my physical limitations. Finally, Mom, remembering the day of my speech a few weeks before, said, "Why don't you call that Lou Carpine? He told you if you needed anything to call him. Maybe he can help you out."

I called Lou, and he invited me to visit him at his office. When I got there we talked about the kinds of work I could do for Sears. After talking to me for a while, Lou told me about a certain position he thought would be perfect for me. He hired me as a catalog order clerk.

It was a great job for me. I worked the hours I wanted and got a better hourly wage than I would have if I'd worked at a fast-food restaurant or a grocery store. My job was to take catalog orders over the phone, record them—on paper when I first started, then later into a computer system—and send them on to be filled. When the incoming orders were slow I would do what they called "outgoings," which was calling people who had ordered things from Sears before, mostly to follow up on their orders and see if Sears could be of any further service.

It was my first real job, and it contributed to my fun, busy life. I would go to school in the morning, work on my cars in the afternoon, then show up at the Sears office and get to work taking orders.

Not only was the job perfect for me, I was perfect for the job. I didn't have to worry about physical limitations getting in the way of doing a good job because the job required only that I be able to answer a phone and converse politely and professionally with the customer. That was never a problem for me, either. I have always been able to converse with anyone, and that made me a hit with the customers.

The job was also a nice fit in that it prepared me for what would lay ahead for me professionally. It was my first real exposure to computers, and that would prove beneficial to me later when I moved into the line of work that would become my career.

MAKING IT IN THE "REAL" WORLD

I was like a lot of new graduates when I left Crestmore High School in the spring of 1980 with diploma in hand: I had no idea what I wanted to do. I'd excelled in auto mechanics and wood and metal shop, but other than that I hadn't specialized in much of anything academically in high school, and I had no real plans for college.

That's a tough time in the lives of a lot of eighteen-year-old kids right out of school. It's a time when they are learning to make their way in a world they aren't used to, a world that doesn't care whether or not they make it, a world their parents had protected them from up to that point. It's the real world, and it can be full of cruel realities.

Life in the real world had the potential to be especially rough on someone like me. Thanks to my father, though, that reality didn't take me totally by surprise. Because of his advice that I would need to use my mind more than my body if I were going to make it in the world of work, I knew there were things I couldn't do for a living. Most blue-collar work—construction, warehouse, and that sort of thing—was out of the question for me.

I also wasn't naïve to the fact that there would be some potential employers who would take a look at me and immediately eliminate me from consideration. I knew I would somehow have to let them find out a little something about me before they did that. I knew it wasn't going to be easy.

But Dad and Mom had instilled in me the attitude that there was a niche for me out there, a place and a profession I could excel in. They were always telling me I had the skills to be president of a company or even a senator. They especially urged me to concentrate on my studies so I could maybe go to law school.

Unlike other recent graduates, when I left high school I wasn't worried about finding a job. I'd been doing it for years, and I somehow knew it wasn't going to stop. I'd always worked and earned money, and I always had a dollar in my pocket. I knew that wasn't the same as earning money, paying rent, and buying food without the safety net of parents. But I guess I thought I was ready to face the rigors of life away from Mom and Dad right away because I didn't wait long after graduation before moving into my own place.

I wasn't thinking in terms of a career when I first got out of high school. I just wanted a decent job to pay my rent, keep my car running, and have some fun with my friends. Since I wasn't in college, it was time for me to get into the world of work.

GETTING WITH THE PROGRAM

It never occurred to me back then that I'd make a career out of the computer field. I did have some experience working on computers at Sears. I knew computers required logic skills, and I was naturally very logical in my thinking.

I got into the computer business when my mother—disappointed I was not pursuing college, let alone a law degree, but knowing I needed a job—called an old friend of hers named Bill Stevens. Bill had started a company in San Jose called Triad Systems, and after Mom called him, she told me to contact him about a position there. I interviewed well and got the job. I worked on computer boards for six months at Triad's manufacturing plant.

But then someone offered me a new adventure.

HOLLYWOOD

I knew some little people in LPA who had appeared in movies, and I got calls from them inquiring about me doing some screen work. It sounded too good to be true.

But it set up a big decision for me. I considered applying for a leave of absence from my job, but since I'd only been there a short time, I didn't think that would work. So I quit to go to Hollywood.

I headed out to Los Angeles to work on a 1981 movie titled *Under the Rainbow*. It starred Chevy Chase and Carrie Fisher. It was a comedy set in 1938, and it had to do with the making of the *Wizard of Oz*. I had a pretty good role in the movie (for an extra), but most of the work I did ended up on the cutting room floor. But I didn't care much because I knew acting wasn't a lifetime goal for me. It was just a fun experience.

My mother was none too pleased I'd left the good job she'd gotten for me. To an adult who has lived in the "real world" for years, it doesn't make sense for a young guy like me to leave a good job, a job that had potential to work into something bigger and better. But to me, appearing in a movie was just too good to pass up. Looking back on it, the move I made wasn't a practical one, but it is a memory I still treasure. Also, it led to some other film appearances later on.

I have appeared in several movies—both on the big screen and in television films. Working on a movie set is very exciting. My short-lived film career gave me many of my fondest memories. I met and appeared (briefly) in movies with a lot of well-known people, including Wilford Brimley, Chevy Chase, Val Kilmer, Carrie Fisher, and Harrison Ford.

There are several little people who have made careers for themselves in movies—I have some friends who have done well in that profession—but for the most part there are few serious roles for little people. That is one of the big complaints, if not *the* big complaint, of many little people. Little people are usually depicted in movies as elves, leprechauns, and gremlins. But we have doctors, lawyers, and other skilled professionals among us. Hollywood needs to portray little people more positively more often.

My biggest claim to fame was when I appeared in *Return of the Jedi*, the third installment in the original *Star Wars* Trilogy. There's no way you would know who I was in the movie if I weren't there to tell you. I appeared in a heavy fur suit as one of the Ewoks, the furry, teddy-bear-like creatures on the forest moon of Endor. And no, my name doesn't appear in the credits. You would recognize Mark Hamill, Harrison Ford, Carrie Fisher, and Billy Dee Williams in their parts, and you'd recognize the voice of James Earl Jones (Darth Vader), but for the most part you wouldn't know one Ewok from another.

Appearing in *Return of the Jedi* was a great experience for me, and it was harder work than you might imagine. We spent long hours on the sets, and when you're on-site for a George Lucas production, there isn't a lot of standing around; the cameras are pretty much always running.

My work on *Return of the Jedi* also led to my "appearance" in a series of lesser-known Ewok movies made for TV (in these, they disguised my crutches as branches). After I got married, my wife, Amy, and I had a little role in *Willow*, a 1988 fantasy movie about an apprentice sorcerer's quest to keep a magical child safe from evil. It starred Val Kilmer, and the title character was played by a little person by the name of Warwick Davis, who has appeared in several other movies. Billy Barty, the founder and former president of Little People of America and a veteran of screen acting, starred in *Willow*.

I returned to the Bay Area from Los Angeles after working on *Under the Rainbow*, needing to find steady work. Fortunately for me, work was plentiful in the area—particularly in a region that came to be known as Silicon Valley. This was the early eighties, and the computer business was booming in the area. There was such a demand for workers—including programmers and software designers—that companies were hiring people with little or no experience, paying for their training, and putting them to work.

BACK TO "REAL" WORK

I was talking to a friend one day not long after my return from Los Angeles, and for some reason I don't remember, he suggested I look into going to school to learn computer programming. It was a nine-month course, and it required that I pass a logic exam, then get a sponsor. I took him up on the idea. I passed the test with a high score and found a sponsor, a man named Floyd Kvamme, the president and founder of a company called National Advanced Systems.

Floyd and his wife, Jeannie, not only sponsored me, they welcomed me to stay at their guest apartment near their own home in San Jose while I attended school. That turned out to be the beginning of a huge break for me.

I frankly wasn't doing very well in programming school. I had the same problem there that I'd had in high school: I just didn't know how to be a good student. One morning as I left my apartment to go to class, I saw Floyd, who needed a ride to work because his car had broken down. I stopped my Volkswagen van and picked him up. On the way to work we chatted about school and the computer business. That was the first time I'd talked much to him, and it turned out to be an important conversation in my life.

When we arrived at Floyd's office at NAS, he asked me in, took me to the personnel department, told me who to talk to, then headed off to work. I talked to the woman in the office, and she asked me what kind of work I liked doing, what I was good at, and when I'd like to start. Before I knew it, I was a junior programmer for National Advanced Systems. A junior programmer was basically an entry-level programmer. I quickly won many of the senior programmers over, and they took me under their wings and taught me much about programming—and corporate politics.

I don't know if anyone can be a "natural" at programming, but that's what seemed to happen after I got the basics down. I didn't have the formal education, but I had the ability to formulate solutions in my head and conceptualize complex problems.

I have some great memories of the first half of the 1980s. Those were some important times in my life with some great memories and a time when the foundation was laid for a good career for me. But they were also times when I underwent the most difficult—and self-imposed—trial of my life.

A TIME OF LEARNING

I would be remiss if I didn't tell you the road to where I am now didn't have some potholes, including some I steered straight into on my own. I made some mistakes along the way. One of those mistakes was that, for a relatively short time in my life, I began experimenting with drugs.

I started smoking things I shouldn't smoke, then worked up to even harder drugs, including cocaine. I didn't get into drugs because of peer pressure or for any escapist reason I'm aware of. I just liked trying different things in life and was stupid enough to go a little further than I knew I should. In the early eighties, drugs were popular and easily available, particularly in a place with as much money floating around as Silicon Valley.

My mom used to visit my apartment from time to time to see if I had food in the fridge. She may not have known for a fact that I was using, but I know she suspected it. I remember her telling me, "Your eyes are glassy. What's going on?" I remember the look of concern on her face, and I remember assuring her that I was fine, that I just wasn't getting enough sleep. She wanted to help, but she knew I had to figure things out on my own. I know now that she spent many hours praying for me.

I never thought I'd be someone who used drugs, but it happened. I thought I could just try it and get out of it, but I was wrong. It caught me like a bear trap. I almost didn't escape.

I never lost a job over it, but it was creating problems for me at work. I ended up in deep debt. I also know that what I was doing was dangerous to my health. I can remember many times when I used drugs how my heart would just pound inside my chest, seemingly trying to break its way through my rib cage. I don't know if the drugs were harder on my body than they would be on an average-sized person's, but I know that I was taking a huge risk using them.

A year or two after I quit, University of Maryland basketball star Len Bias, who had just been drafted by the Boston Celtics, died of cocaine-related causes. That was a true tragedy for a young man to die that way, and I am grateful I didn't meet the same fate.

I know I wasted a lot of time, a lot of energy, and a lot of money on my habit. More importantly, I knew God was disappointed in my decisions. He had been doing so much for me—giving me my job, my apartment, my friends—and here I was, putting it all in jeopardy.

I wanted to quit, but couldn't. At times I would open my Bible to look for some strength and wisdom. I found a place in the book of Romans where it talks about why we do things we don't want to do (Romans 7). I asked God, *What am I doing? I don't want to be in this state! Why am I here?* I'd pray for the strength to stop using, and I'd be okay for a few days, but then I'd make the choice to start doing it again.

I am happy to report I quit using drugs before I did any major damage to my mind or body. It wasn't a big, miraculous delivery from addiction for me. More than anything, drugs were replaced by other things in my life. I stopped using them, quit associating with the people who got me started on them, started hanging out with people who didn't do those kinds of things, and started a new job.

The saying, "Once an addict, always an addict" applies here. I am an addictive-type personality. I know if I were to spend prolonged periods with drug users, I would probably step into that trap again. I've just got to be sure I don't get back into that crowd. Plus, I've lost interest in that lifestyle. I've got so many healthy things going on—and so many painful memories from that time—that I don't *want* to go back there.

When I was at National Advanced Systems, I dated a senior programmer named Joy. Joy could be tough with me and speak truthfully. "Matt, you need to knock this off," she told me. "You are going downhill with this stuff and you need to quit." She encouraged me to attend group meetings with her, and I did. I don't know if they did me as much good as just having a friend like Joy.

I also got a lot of help from my grandmother, who helped me get my finances back in order by basically managing my money until I was out of the debt I had accrued during my time of drug use.

I learned a lot about God during that time in my life. I learned that God gives you choices. He won't force you to choose the right thing. He'll make right and wrong clear, but it's up to you to decide your course.

MAKING SOMETHING GOOD OUT OF A BAD TIME

I've always believed good things can come from trying and bad experiences. I'm not suggesting someone should go out and use drugs or anything, but I know positive things can come from times when we drift off course.

I wondered for many years how my drug use could be used as a good thing. I understand now my experiences can help me relate to someone who is making the same mistakes. I can now look someone in the eye and say, "I've been there, and you're headed to no place good. You need to do whatever it takes to stop." Now I tell anyone who is tinkering with drugs to stay away from it. If someone offers it to you, run—don't walk—away.

About the time I got away from the drugs—and the influences that could have led me back to drug use—I started on a new direction in my work life.

A TURN IN THE ROAD

I was grateful for the opportunity I had to start my computer career at National Advanced Systems. I really thought I would stay there for the long run. But I didn't understand that computer programmers were a transient type of worker. They would start at one company, learn more about the business, then move on to another company to start off at a higher position. After almost two years at NAS, that's what happened to me. For a time, I made the rounds in Silicon Valley, moving from job to job several times. Because of the demand for programmers, I was never unemployed for even a full day.

Eventually, I ended up at Altos Computer Systems, where my career really started to take off. I was working on some projects that were at the time on the cutting edge of computer technology. I've always been able to think somewhat ahead of the pack and develop new ideas and techniques to make better programs and solve real business problems.

I was also extremely resourceful. It's one thing to have a great new idea; it's another to know how to get it done without costing the company a fortune. Budgets and corporate earnings are everything. If somebody else in our company wrote some good code which might be adapted for one of my projects, I was interested in using it. My objective was to deliver the best product as quickly and cost-effectively as possible. If that meant building on other people's ideas, great. Many of my own solutions were being adapted by others, so it worked for everyone.

I first started pulling away from the pack as a designer at Altos when my team employed what at that time was a very advanced yet simple database design technique. It's called *normalization*. If you want to hear the technical details, here they are: We took normalization a step further by dynamically synthesizing volatile attributes with static tables of normalized data. A practical technique useful today in many business applications.

I started to notice I was becoming more valuable to the company—I suddenly got assigned a big office with a floor to ceiling window (a cherished thing in a building full of cubicles), and my salary kept going up.

One time I had this great idea for an application, but my bosses couldn't really catch the vision because it was all so conceptual. I knew what they needed was a working model. I worked on my regular projects during the day, but at night I'd work on my own idea.

Finally, I finished my prototype. It worked just the way I'd envisioned it. It was ready for prime time. I showed it to the senior managers. They were interested. They told me to show it to the vice president. He took one look at it and said, "Let's go with it." We installed it on the network. Three weeks later at a company meeting, the VP called me up to the front to accept an award. "If I had two more people like Matt," he said, "I could rule the world."

I worked on several other projects on my own time like that—some of them are still used in computer programming today. I always had more innovative ideas than could be explored in a lifetime. Whenever I'd ask if I could work on something radically new, my boss would say, "Here's the rope, go hang yourself."

I had a great boss for the kind of things I was doing. His name was Jon Andreasen, an old navy petty officer. He was a no-nonsense, no-frills kind of boss that everybody loved. In the office, he was very gruff in how he communicated with employees. After work, he'd go out and socialize with those same people. When you walked into his office, he'd look up and ask, "What do you need?" and you'd have to get to the point immediately or you'd lose him. After you stated your case, he'd say either yes or no with no real explanation outside of "I don't think that's a good idea."

Jon Andreasen wasn't one to voice how he appreciated my efforts, but I still got recognition and reward for my work. After a time at Altos, I was moved around and up until I was basically running the show in my department. Here I was, one of the least qualified, least educated employees at Altos, and I was being moved up. All because I was willing to give a little extra.

To me, there's a message in this story. I hear people all the time who want to move ahead in their line of work, but I also hear them say, "How can I do it? I have a great idea, but my boss won't let me do it." I learned that it doesn't hurt sometimes when you go home, to turn off the TV, sit down, and work on some ideas of your own.

I did that, and it enhanced my professional life. It moved me from one level of my line of work to the next. I made an impression by going the extra mile, by doing more than was expected or required of me.

In fact, there was a time when my bosses started to think I was working too hard and too long for my own good. It was that observation that led to an introduction to one very important person in my life.

FINDING LOVE AS A LITTLE PERSON

L ike any other group in the world, little people meet, fall in love, marry, have children, and grow old together.

Although I had dated some average-sized women and formed some wonderful relationships along the way, I always wanted to marry a little person. Most little people end up marrying other little people. (There are exceptions—my brother Sam married an average-sized woman, and they have a happy marriage and a child.) I also knew I would marry a woman who shared my beliefs and values. But even if I could find a woman who was both a little person and a Christian, it wouldn't mean she and I would be compatible in other areas.

Talk about a needle in a haystack! Talk about narrowing the field! I was looking for a woman with so many specific attributes that I wondered if she even existed. But I also had faith that God's plan would unfold for me in time just as it had in so many areas in my life.

FINDING TIME FOR LOVE

There was another problem: I was so into my work I had little time for anything else. I was the very epitome of the word *workaholic*. In 1986 I was working incredibly long hours at Altos Computer Systems. Work weeks of eighty-five hours were not uncommon for me, and I had many weeks of one hundred plus hours. Often, I'd work my regular day shift, say good night to everyone when they went home for the night, then say good morning to them when they arrived for work the next day. I'd work all night, stopping only for a bite to eat, a cup of coffee, or to change into the spare pair of socks I had in my desk drawer.

It was crazy how many hours I worked. I know there's no way I could survive like that now. I often work long hours as it is, but I know my body and mind—not to mention my marriage and relationship with my children—would break down if I tried that now.

It was kind of an ego thing for me. This was the first job in which I was running the show. I had some programmers assisting me, but I was in charge. I had management-type duties, too: budgets and schedules and all sorts of things.

I seemed to thrive on what now seems like an impossible work schedule. I got great satisfaction from designing programs, then seeing them used. One analyst wrote about my programs that they were successful because they were innovative, simple, and user-friendly. To a program designer, there's no higher compliment than to say his programs are effective and easy to use. I also felt good that the work I was doing had a positive impact on the company's bottom line.

It didn't seem like I'd ever wind down or even need time off. I had quit using drugs and my life was headed in the right direction. I worked that much simply because I liked it. I wasn't trying to overcompensate for anything; I just liked the work I was doing and enjoyed being a star employee.

Finally, my bosses had seen enough. They appreciated my willingness to work all the overtime it took me to get the job done, but they knew I needed a break. They knew it wasn't wise to have a worker—even a willing one like me—spend that much time in the office. They wanted me to take some time off, and they had just the thing for me to do. They wanted me to go to the Little People of America convention that July in Dearborn, Michigan, a suburb of Detroit.

"I don't have time for that!" I protested. "I have too much code to bang out." It was the typical workaholic's response to the idea of relaxing and taking some time for himself.

But it didn't wash with my bosses. In a move they would one day come to regret, my bosses got together and paid for my trip. They paid for my admission to the conference, airfare to and from, and my lodging in Detroit. I'm sure if they'd had to, they would have packed my bags for me, hog-tied me, and deposited me at the gate to catch the plane. Finally, I gave in—provided I could take some work documents along in case I found time.

Despite my objections, I knew I would have a good time at the convention. I had been active in the LPA, so the trip would give me the chance to see old friends and catch up on LPA news.

That convention changed my life. And the life of one little lady who happened to live in Detroit.

OVERCOMING SOME AWKWARDNESS

She almost didn't come. Amy Knight lived in Westland, Michigan, a short drive from the convention hotel. While I had attended several national LPA conventions prior to 1986, this was Amy's first. Although she would grow to enjoy herself at the convention, it was difficult for her at first.

Amy was painfully shy growing up with her parents, Gordon and Patricia Knight, and her brother and two sisters. She was around five years old when she realized she was different from her siblings and the other children she knew. Often, it was hard for her to even walk by a mirror and see how small she was, how different her body looked from other girls her age. As she grew into her teens, social situations—those situations some teenagers thrive in—became terribly awkward for her.

Amy liked boys and wanted to date. But she didn't, simply because she wasn't asked out. Her first date was at age seventeen, and it was a disaster. She went out with a little person she had met through LPA, and both of them were so shy they barely spoke.

After high school, Amy headed to Mt. Pleasant, Michigan, to attend Central Michigan University. Although college is a place where even the most shy people can meet people and make friends, her social life didn't improve. She even had a difficult time taking part in conversations with the other girls in her college dorm. She just didn't live the same life they did. They would talk about who they dated or guys they had met, and she had nothing to add to the conversation.

When you meet her now, it's hard to believe Amy ever struggled with being little. She can be a little shy in some situations, but overall she's a strong woman who isn't afraid to assert herself when she needs to. Amy sometimes felt sorry for herself because she didn't feel like she fit in. She has told me several times that only her faith in God kept her believing she would meet someone one day.

After graduating from college in May of 1985, Amy went to work as a secretary at a window washing company. It wasn't her idea of a "dream job" or even what she wanted to do in the long run, but it was a job. She worked there while she looked for something she really wanted to do.

But what Amy really wanted was something that no job—no matter how prestigious and high paying it might be—could offer. Since the time she was a little girl, Amy wanted to be married and to have children. The problem was she didn't know how to make those things a reality in her life.

Like me, Amy knew she would marry a little person. It wasn't that she was limiting herself to that option; it was simple pragmatism. She had never been asked out by an average-sized man, and she knew it wasn't common for a dwarf to marry a tall person. A lot of that, she knew, was due to bigotry on both sides. Many tall people would look at average-sized people marrying a little person as truly bizarre, and, likewise, many little people didn't look at marrying a tall person with great favor.

So how was Amy going to find someone? How could she make a connection with another little person when little people were so spread out and hard to meet?

Some of Amy's friends suggested she attend the LPA convention. It made sense to them: the biggest meeting of little people in the nation was going to be held in her own hometown. She wouldn't have to pay for airfare, a hotel, or anything else. It was a no-risk situation for her. All she had to do was show up. If she really hated it, she could go home.

Amy is a very practical, sensible woman, and it seemed that going to the LPA convention would be a practical way to meet some other little people. She knew that just being there didn't guarantee she'd even make friends, much less meet a nice guy. Really, the only thing an LPA convention does is bring together people with one thing in common: they're short. Beyond that, it's up to each individual what he or she does with the time at the convention.

The convention required her to make an adjustment. Amy isn't the "mixer" I am. I've always been the kind of person who can walk up to people I don't even know and start a conversation. Not Amy. She most definitely has a warm, conversational side to her, but she has a difficult time engaging in chitchat with people she doesn't know. On top of that, many of the convention attendees already knew each other. It also took her some time to adjust to being around so many little people. At first, she felt like an outsider.

She attended some of the events—seminars, athletic events, workshops, social meetings—at the convention, and started meeting people. She began to feel something she'd never felt before: a sense of belonging. For the first time in her life, she was around people who were like her, who endured the same problems she did, and who had the same sense of frustration from an average-sized world. For once, she felt accepted as a human being, and not as some kind of human novelty. She started making real friends, lasting friends, friends with whom she has remained close to this day.

And, I'm happy to say, one of those was me.

MEETING AMY

I wasn't looking for a wife when I went to the 1986 LPA convention. It's not that I had anything against the idea of marriage. I just wasn't in a hurry. Still, I knew I would have a chance to meet some little women at the convention. I at least looked forward to making some very nice acquaintances. I met Amy early in the convention week through an interest we shared: sports.

Each of the LPA conventions has competitive sports events among its activities. Volleyball, basketball, weight lifting, and several others. I first saw Amy at the weight lifting competition just a day or two into the convention. I wasn't lifting that year—I was working too much, and not working *out* enough. I was there sizing up the competition for next year. Amy was watching the event. We first saw each other when I came in the room and sat down to watch.

Soon, Amy and I gravitated toward one another. We started talking about our work, our families, our friends. It didn't take long before I realized we had lots of mutual interests—not to mention mutual attraction. As I talked to her, I knew I wanted to get to know her better. She felt the same way.

I saw Amy several times that week, including at the basketball finals. I sat with a friend, Peter Reckendorf, and watched her play. She was playing with a group of guys she knew from her local LPA chapter. I was impressed by her competitiveness, her demeanor, and how she related to the other players—not to mention her skill. Here she was playing in the gold medal game with all these guys, and she was a dominant player. At one point she made a basket from half court. It was at that moment I knew she was interesting.

It turns out Amy is an amazing athlete. If she's not the top female athlete in the LPA, she's in the top five. These days, she always gets asked to play on the best teams at our national conventions. Her sisters were very athletic, and her brother was an outstanding high school swimmer who later went on to swim competitively at the college level. Amy was a fantastic basketball player. She also played volleyball. She's been on several gold-medal-winning teams over the years.

When I saw her sink that basket, I leaned over and asked Peter if he knew Amy. But he wasn't much better acquainted with her than I was. She was new to the LPA national scene, so not many people there knew a whole lot about her. I was going to have to find out more on my own.

The convention ended with a banquet. It was a dressy affair, and Amy looked great. She had on this amazing evening gown. Without a doubt, she was the most attractive woman at the ball. She was a knockout.

The only problem was that she wasn't with me. She had been asked to the banquet by another guy at the convention. His name was Danny. I was with a girl named Camille. It's amazing how many times Amy and I "accidentally" bumped into each other that night. We took as many chances to be with each other at the banquet that we could. (I think Danny and Camille must've been doing the same thing on the other side of the banquet room because they were married several months later.) Amy and I talked about staying in touch when we went our separate ways. We exchanged addresses and phone numbers.

The next day I headed back to northern California, anxious to get back to work. I wasn't sure what I was going to do about Amy. I knew I liked her, but I also knew she lived in Detroit, half a continent away from me. It was going to be interesting to see how, and if, this spark we'd ignited would flame or go out.

STAYING IN TOUCH

Less than a week after I got back to San Jose—I was already back into my ninety-hour-a-week grind—I got a letter from Amy. It wasn't a love letter, just a nice note telling me how she enjoyed meeting me and getting acquainted at the convention. Those feelings were mutual, and I had every intention of writing back and telling her so...just as soon as I had a little time.

Amy told me later that she was a little miffed that I didn't write back right away. She was interested in starting a relationship with me, but she also knew the long-distance nature of the thing required I put in the effort, too. I wanted to stay in contact, but I was—and still am—a pretty lousy letter writer. Put me with someone in person, or even on the phone, and I do fine. But if I have to resort to letter writing, it can be a struggle.

Amy's attitude was that if I didn't want to write back or call her, life would go on. It was my loss, after all. Here she was, just what I was looking for: a beautiful, intelligent, level-headed, athletic little woman—and a Christian to boot. My needle in the haystack. What was my problem?

Not long after her first letter, Amy wrote again. To this day, Amy has no idea what motivated her to write again. Ordinarily, if someone didn't take the time to return her correspondence, that would have been the end of it. The tone of the second letter suggested that if I were interested in her, I'd better do something about it. If not...well, it was nice meeting you.

Instead of writing back, I called her. Our first phone conversation was mostly small talk. From there, our phone calls became more and more regular. She often called me from Detroit at five in the morning my time—at the office, of course. I was back to working the crazy all-day, all-night shifts, so she knew where to find me. She'd talk to me while I worked away in front of my computer screen.

After writing back and forth and talking on the phone for several months, we arranged for Amy to come to California to visit me. Actually, it was Amy who took the first step. She had some vacation time coming, and she was going to come to California to visit a friend who lived about an hour from me. Amy called and suggested she stop by to see me.

"Sure, that's great!" I told her. "I'd love to see you. I'll show you around when you get here."

I was looking forward to getting to know her away from the surroundings of the LPA convention, where—like any social gathering—people put on their best faces. We were going to spend time together alone, and I knew this would be a chance for us to get to know each other as we really were. When it's just the two of us, we'd really have to communicate, and I was looking forward to finding out how well we'd do in a situation like that.

Amy told me she was going to come visit for a day, then head up to Sacramento to see her friend. So as our first day drew to an end, I asked if she needed to call her friend. She said, "No, I can actually stay another day, I think." Great, I thought. A flexible schedule. The next day I asked her the same thing—and got the same answer. In the end, she spent the whole week with me and never visited her friend at all.

Looking back on it, I think that was her plan all along. I think she had her friend on standby, like maybe she called her and said, "I'm going to visit this guy. If it doesn't work out, I'm coming to your house. If it does work out, maybe you won't see me this trip." I think she snuck into the next room every afternoon to call her friend and tell her she wasn't coming that day. Each of these nights, I followed through as I'd promised on the phone—sleeping on the couch and giving Amy my bedroom.

That week we spent together is still one our fondest memories. I took Amy all over the San Francisco Bay area. We toured the Napa Valley wine country, had picnics on the beach, and ate dinners in fancy restaurants. I can't remember having such a good time talking with someone. The time just flew by when we were together, and we were never at a loss for something to talk about. We were both amazed at how comfortable we were around one another.

I made a special effort to give Amy a full appreciation for my favorite spot on the planet: the Golden Gate Bridge. I showed her that bridge from every angle possible. She loved it.

I guess the bridge is so special to me because of one particular childhood

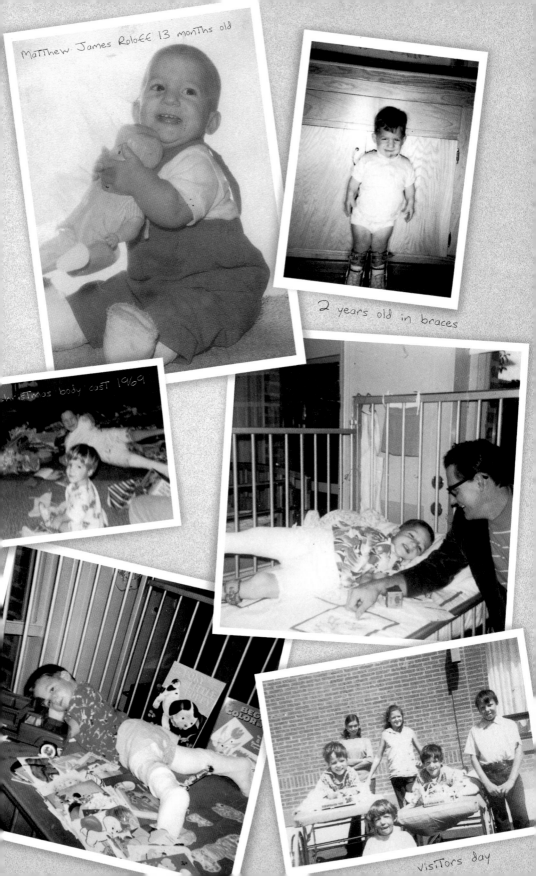

Matthew James Roloff 13 months old

2 years old in braces

Christmus body cast 1969

Visitors day

growing up on the farm

2nd place winner,
slowest bike race, 1976

Matt skiing, 1978

The family, 1977
atop Glacier Point

The boys got their own ATV's at age 4 and were riding solo by age 5

Twins Jeremy and Zachery one big, one little.

Molly painting her 2-story playhouse

restoring The 100 year old barn

maTT wiTh his Track hoe
Amy hard aT work on The TracTor

The Roloff family Tree house, built from reclaimed barn lumber and old Telephone poles, has 4 levels, 6 meThods of access and is compleTely self-supporTing.

The 24' pirate ship has secret connection passage-ways, bunkbeds, captain's and crew quarters and a gang plank.

ROLLY POLLY

many groups come and enjoy The RoloFF Farm

The old West Tow...
includes over 300
of secret undergro...
Tunnels

The mine shaft goes
back 70' under The
red barn To a secret
Trap door

memory. Josh was in a crucial surgery, literally struggling for his life. We thought we were going to lose him this time. It was open-heart surgery and it was going to take six hours, so Dad bundled us up in our coats and took us on a long, slow walk across the Golden Gate Bridge. I remember how the cold fog felt so refreshing to our spirits.

And now, to see Amy loving this bridge as much as I did…it just spoke to me. I knew she was the one.

I took her to meet Mom and Dad, as well as my sister, my brother, and my grandmother. Amy was a little uncomfortable meeting them, especially since we'd only known one another a short time ourselves. I wasn't taking Amy to meet my family just because I thought they'd enjoy meeting my new "friend." I wanted to know what they thought of her, if they believed she could be the woman I should marry. Not surprisingly, my whole family loved her.

Before we knew it, our week together was over. It was time for Amy to head back to Detroit, and me back to my long hours on the job.

WHAT NEXT?

There was no question in our minds at the end of that week that we wanted to keep seeing one another. I sent Amy a dozen roses, which she received her first day back to work. From that time forward, we talked on the phone nearly every day.

Now it was my turn to make the big step of going to Detroit to meet Amy's family. That April, a month after she had come to see me in California, I flew out to stay with Amy and her family for five days.

Amy was nervous about my coming to stay with her family. She wanted so much for them to like me. I think they thought of me as a little wild and untamed. Then there were their natural concerns arising from the fact that I needed crutches to get around. But if there was a wild side to me, it certainly didn't show when I was in Detroit. I'd just come off a major work project, and I was exhausted. For the first several days, I slept in. During the visit, I took the opportunity to visit one-on-one with each member of Amy's family. All their misgivings were soon put to rest, and we had their blessing to continue in our relationship.

Amy and I both knew our relationship could be headed for marriage. The question for us was when we'd make that step and how we'd do it. During her first visit to California, I'd asked Amy if she would be willing to move to northern California to be with me. When I'd asked her that, it was in more of a hypothetical, "what if" way. That didn't sit well with Amy. She wanted more than a hypothetical; she wanted a commitment, and there was no way she was going to move out to California without one. She wanted to know I was serious about making her my wife.

Amy had decided long before she met me that if she found the right guy, it wouldn't matter where he lived. Moving or not moving wasn't an issue to her. That seemed so trivial to her compared with the idea of spending the rest of her life with someone. She knew she would work it out.

I knew I wanted to marry Amy, and I knew that if she had a commitment from me she would be willing to move to California. Now it was time for me to take a big step, one of the biggest I've ever taken.

GETTING ENGAGED

My heart was pounding. My blood pressure was up. I wondered if I could go through with it that day.

I'm not talking about my plans to ask Amy to marry me; I'm talking about our visit to the top of Glacier Point at Yosemite National Park.

A month after my visit to Detroit, Amy came to California to visit with me for another week. I was prepared to pop the question—I had my grand-mother's ring in my pocket, ready to slip it on Amy's finger—but my fear of heights (high places are one of the few things that really scare me) made it a nerve-wracking day. Amy wanted to walk to the edge of the bluff and look down at the scenery. I'll admit it was beautiful, but I couldn't go over there. I kept asking her to come back to me, away from the edge of the cliff. At first Amy teased me about it. At that point, I don't think she understood my fear of heights. She just wanted me to see the scenery up close.

Finally, after some coaxing, I got her to come sit with me—away from the edge. It was my moment. (I'd had some friends give me some good advice. They said, "Matt, pop the question, then shut up. Don't keep talking like you always do.") I pulled out the little box in my pocket, opened it to expose the ring, and said, "Amy, I love you. Will you marry me?" (Then I zipped my lip and waited for her answer.) With tears in her eyes, she said yes. Soon both of us were crying. I slipped the ring on her finger, and it was official.

THE WEDDING DAY

I didn't want to wait to get married. I wanted to elope. That sounded like an adventure. I wanted to leave for our honeymoon, then come back and have a reception for the family. But Amy wouldn't budge. Like so many young girls, she had dreamed her whole life of her wedding day, and she wasn't going to be cheated out of it. She left me in California and went back to Michigan, where she got busy planning our wedding.

We had planned an October wedding, but, at my insistence, we moved it up to September 12. We were married at Aldersgate United Methodist Church, the church in which Amy grew up.

Appropriately, we spent our wedding night at the hotel which had been the site of the LPA convention where we'd met. Then we flew to California and honeymooned in Carmel. After our honeymoon, we held a reception for all my friends and family in California.

It was a great beginning to our life together, a life that would shortly take several new turns.

TAKING SOME RISKS

10

As well matched as Amy and I are for one another, as great a wife as she has been to me, as well as we seem to fit one another—we are quite different in our personalities in a number of ways, not the least of which is in how we approach risks in life.

Amy is Miss Practical and Sensible, while I'm the one who is always looking for adventures. Amy is the one who wants things planned out, while I'm the one who is just as content to roll with whatever comes my way.

I don't want to leave the impression that I'm a risk taker to the point of being reckless. I would never risk my wife's or kids' security, no matter what the potential payoff. While I believe part of what makes life exciting and enjoyable is taking risks, I also believe in taking *calculated* risks: risks in which you weigh what you could lose if your risk doesn't pay off against what you could gain if it does, then decide if it's worth doing.

I took a risk like that shortly after Amy and I got married: I quit my well-paying, secure job at Altos Computer Systems. I see that as a great example of a calculated risk because I knew from past experience and my work history that I wasn't risking being able to pay the rent and put food on the table for Amy and me. There was no question in my mind I could find a job that would more than cover our costs of living.

I didn't take this risk because I thought I could find a higher-paying job or a more prestigious position. I was more than content on both fronts in the job I had. This risk came because I wanted a change, and the biggest part of that was I was a newlywed.

I quit my job at Altos because I wanted to spend time with my new bride. I told my bosses I needed to cut back on my hours, that I couldn't work all night long anymore now that I was married. I asked for some relief in the hours I was working. Although they agreed, Altos had a hard time making that transition. They had gotten used to me being willing to work insanely long hours. (I'm sure they regretted sending me to that convention.) It wasn't long before I realized I'd set a precedent that couldn't easily be broken. I knew I would need to move on if I wanted to work more "normal" hours.

I gave notice at Altos, and I left on good terms, still friends with everyone there. It was time for a new chapter in my professional life.

WORKING TILL OREGON

I had received employment offers from companies all over Silicon Valley while I was at Altos. Some of them were from large companies, others from little family businesses.

One of the offers was from 3Com. I went straight to work for them when I left Altos. I was doing the same thing at 3Com I had done at Altos: designing service applications. It wasn't more than two months until I realized 3Com wasn't where I wanted to be, so I quit and went to work for Fairfax-Roe, a small consulting firm.

At Fairfax-Roe, I got away from the design and got more into the business side of my line of work. I did well, too, because I had a lot of contacts from my time at Altos. I just sent out mailers to the people I knew and waited for the business to come in.

I was bringing in all kinds of business for Fairfax-Roe, and it soon occurred to me that I could do the kind of work I was doing for them on my own and make more money doing it. I left Fairfax-Roe and developed my own consulting business. I liked the freedom of working for myself, but I soon found that my personality wasn't suited for self-employment. I'm not the most focused, disciplined person in the world.

I was still getting calls from businesses wanting to hire me, and I decided to take a job with Arix Computer Systems in San Jose. That was a memorable job because I was there when the Bay Area was hit by the World Series Quake of 1989 (so named because it struck just before the third game of the World Series between the Oakland Athletics and the San Francisco Giants).

I stayed at Arix for almost a year, and it was the first time since Amy and I had been married that I had what she would have considered some job stability. We were never hurting for money because I was earning a good living and Amy was in a well-paying job at Hewlett-Packard. But I know Amy started to wonder if I would ever settle down and stay with one job for any length of time. When we got married, I had been at Altos for nearly four years, but now that I was married, it seemed I couldn't settle down.

I had saved some money from my consulting business. That, coupled with our two incomes, gave Amy and me the opportunity to buy our first house together. It was a lovely, brand-new house in a very nice neighborhood in San Jose. We were able to be first-time home owners at a time when it was almost impossible for young couples to afford a home in San Jose, let alone one as nice as ours. It appeared that we would be settling down for the long run.

That was when someone presented me with an idea that would change my life, an idea I thought was crazy at first, but an idea that grew on me.

I was content working at Arix. I was making good money, and I had no intention of going anywhere. One day, though, Pat Guinn, a friend and coworker from my days at Altos, walked into my home office and announced his plans to move to the Pacific Northwest.

"Matt, I'm moving to Oregon," he said, the enthusiasm shining through his eyes. "I've found a job at a computer company, and I'm going to live in Oregon."

"Oregon!" I said. "Pat, why in the world would you move to Oregon? What's in Oregon?"

As Pat left my office, I remember thinking *Good luck, you fool!* I couldn't understand why anyone would want to leave the center of the universe for high technology—Silicon Valley—to move to a place like Oregon. When I thought of Oregon, I thought of the backwoods: the type of place you'd want to visit for a camping or fishing trip, but not a place you'd want to live. *Beautiful, but too desolate,* I thought. What Hollywood is to actors, Silicon

Valley is to computer professionals. To me, Oregon wasn't even on the map.

Pat didn't share my cynicism. He went through with his move to the Portland area and went to work for Sequent Computer Systems, a large, well-respected company in a suburb of Portland. About three months later, Pat called me. He raved about the Oregon area, telling me about the physical beauty of the place and about the people, who, he said, were as friendly as any you could ever meet. He also told me that there would be a job waiting for me if I wanted to move there.

"Matt, Sequent needs you," he said. Pat had appointed himself my walking, talking résumé with his bosses, and they were interested.

"Pat, you know how I work," I said. "I need room to be innovative. I can't fight some system. I can't work for a company that's not thinking out of the box."

"Matt, trust me."

The people at Sequent called me and asked me if I'd at least come for a visit. They offered to pay for everything, so there would be no risk to me. Finally, after a few more phone calls from Pat and his bosses, I was persuaded to at least check out the place. I respected Pat, and I knew Oregon must have something going for it for him to talk about it that way. If nothing else, it would be a chance to visit my friend.

When I saw the area and what Sequent was offering me, it was love at first sight. The people there rolled out the red carpet for me. I could tell they really wanted me. Pat showed me around the Portland area, and, just as he'd promised, I was struck with its beauty and how friendly the people were. I fell in love with it instantly.

It was hard for me not to be enthusiastic about this opportunity. I'd been offered a job with an up-and-coming company doing what I do best: working on service systems. The money was right, and I loved the area. I knew what I wanted to do, but I had to make sure I had Amy's approval before we'd make a move like that.

Amy was a little nervous about relocating, mostly because she wondered what would happen to us if the job at Sequent didn't work out. But the practical side of her saw the benefits of moving to Oregon. We could get a larger home for much less money (the housing costs in the Silicon Valley were astronomical), and it was in an area where we'd want to raise children.

I brought Amy up to check out the area and to look at the housing situation there. With that, she gave her approval. I decided to come back to Oregon to look for a house in earnest.

There was a complication, though, a rather important detail we needed to see to before we finalized our plans. We needed to look into health care for Amy because she was pregnant. With twins.

ONE FINAL DETAIL

Amy and I knew from the time the thoughts of marriage started that we wanted at least three children. With her expecting twins, we were about to be two-thirds of the way there.

The doctors at San Jose Medical Center told us almost at the beginning that Amy was expecting two babies. They were excited to take on a fairly rare case like a little person expecting twins. Twins are pretty unusual for little people. Amy and I know a lot of little people, and we know *of* a lot of others, and we have heard of only two other little women who have had twins.

Amy's pregnancy was high risk and routine at the same time. It was high risk simply because all pregnancies in little women are automatically placed in that category. It's not that little women can't safely carry children; they certainly can. But there are risk factors, among them being the smaller size of their pelvic area. That makes cesarean section an automatic for little women. Amy's pregnancy was all the more high risk because it was with twins. But she was determined to carry these babies as long as necessary for a healthy delivery.

When we were thinking about moving, we wanted to make certain Amy would have the same quality of care in Portland she had in San Jose. We called around, asked questions, and got references. We looked for the right doctors for this unusual case. The problem was that so few doctors anywhere had seen anything like this. When I talked to different doctors, I found that most believed they could handle the case, despite the fact that so few of them had worked with little people, particularly a little person who was pregnant with twins. It seemed most of them looked at this case as a challenge and something they hadn't done before. That's what I wanted to hear.

As someone who likes challenges, I think that if a doctor doesn't want a challenge, he or she should probably go into another line of work. Still, I was concerned more with the doctor's qualifications than his or her willingness and enthusiasm to take our case.

We visited with the doctors and staff at Emanuel Hospital in Portland. It was a beautiful, newly-restored hospital, and we were impressed with the qualifications and attitude of the doctors there. After our visit to Emanuel, we were confident Amy would receive outstanding care if we moved. That was all we needed to know. We accepted Sequent's offer.

FINDING A DREAM HOME

Moving from one home to another isn't easy. It's especially intimidating to a guy who has trouble moving his chair up to the table for supper, let alone moving it onto a truck.

When Amy and I came to Oregon to look for a home, we found several good candidates and finally purchased one, though none had totally grabbed us. Then, with our earnest money locked up, we saw it: a thirty-four-acre farm that had been on the market for some time. The realtor who had it listed claimed several people in the computer industry in the area were interested in it.

The realtor drove us around the farm so we could check it out. To say it wasn't much to look at is an understatement. It was at the end of a long, bumpy driveway—no fun for Amy, who could feel the twins bouncing around in her belly. The farm wasn't much better than the one on *Green Acres*. Most of the land was overgrown with thistles and wild blackberries. The house was a mess. This wasn't just one of those "a little paint and a few flowers" projects, either. It would take major work to get this place livable.

I found out a lot of potential buyers had turned up their noses at this place just because of the way the house looked. Most people looked at it and saw a dump, but I saw a diamond in the rough. I loved the contour of the land, and the location was prime. Even the house had some potential. I looked at this place and had a hunch it could be something special.

I had learned how to see potential in a home like that from my mother. Mom could walk into the crummiest, nastiest, most run-down looking place around—the kind of house most people would expect to be condemned—and with some paint, some cleaning utensils, some yard tools, and a lot of elbow grease, turn it into something beautiful. She'd rip out everything that needed to go, then replace it with what needed to be there.

It was as if I not only wanted to buy a farm, I wanted to take on a challenge with this place. I talked money with the realtor and worked the price to where I wanted it. Now it was time to persuade Amy.

"Honey, I know this place doesn't look so great," I said, "but I know this could be something special. I love the lay of the land here. We can even do something with the house. And look at all this land—our kids will have room to run."

I think that's what clinched it for her. Besides, she was in no mood to argue. She was tired from the whole resettlement process, and she just wanted to lie down. "It looks great," she said. "Do what you think is best for us."

We backed out of the other deal—losing some of our earnest money—and purchased the farm. We immediately contracted some work on it, just to get it livable enough for us to move in. Then we went back to San Jose to pack.

My friends from Silicon Valley threw us a big send-off party, and there was even a little article in the *San Jose Mercury News* about my departure. I knew I would miss my friends in the area, but I looked forward to the challenges ahead for me and Amy. I had so many plans for the farm: a working orchard, a restored barn, a paved tricycle track for the twins. I couldn't wait to get started.

Oh yes, the twins. In the midst of all that, I was about to embark on one of the grandest adventures of my life: fatherhood. The question was, would I be the father of someone like Amy and me, a little person?

We knew the chances of that happening were pretty good, and up until the final trimester of Amy's pregnancy, we were still waiting for the answer.

ARE THEY, OR AREN'T THEY?

Although Amy's pregnancy was high risk, we were told up front there was no reason to be overly concerned because Amy was healthy. With her being in the high-risk category, we were able to get her extra medical attention without having to worry about whether our insurance would cover it. The doctors watched Amy closely throughout the pregnancy. We had ultrasounds every two or three weeks, and each time, the doctor told us, "You're looking good, see you in a couple weeks."

We knew from the beginning we had a good chance of parenting a little person, but not a diastrophic, the kind of dwarf I am. For example, a baby born to two achondroplastic dwarfs (like Amy) has a 25 percent chance of being average-sized, a 50 percent chance of being a dwarf like its parents, and a 25 percent chance of being born with what is called a double-dominant gene, which is a pretty hopeless situation because the child invariably dies at birth or shortly thereafter.

Fortunately for us, we didn't have to worry about all that because I am a diastrophic dwarf and Amy is achondroplastac. That meant that if we had a child who was a little person, he or she would be an achondroplastac dwarf because the gene for that condition is a dominant one. We were told that the odds of one of our children being born a diastrophic were pretty remote because diastrophics don't generally have diastrophic offspring.

Amy and I talked a lot during the early stages of her pregnancy about how we would handle it if one or both of the babies were a little person. We talked about three scenarios: two average-sized kids, one average-sized and one dwarf, and two dwarfs. We talked about the inherent problems with raising dwarf children, something both of us knew about intimately. We also talked about what it would be like to raise two average-sized children as dwarf parents, something many of our friends had to handle because children of dwarfs are commonly average-sized.

While Amy and I both knew the problems—social and otherwise—little people face, we were comfortable with the possibility that one or both of our children could be little. The way we saw it, if they were little, we'd be prepared to be the best parents any two dwarf children could have, simply because we could empathize with the things they dealt with in a world full of tall people. If they were average-sized, we were ready to raise a family in which the children were taller than the parents before their tenth birthdays.

Our doctors watched the babies' growth closely, using ultrasound pictures to chart their bone growth to see if it was progressing normally. This was different than most people's pregnancies because it's very rare that a doctor would even look for dwarfism in a fetus. At about the six-month mark, an ultrasound photo showed it: One of the babies' bone growth had tailed off. We were going to be the parents of at least one little person.

On May 10, 1990, Amy and I became parents of two baby boys: Jeremy, an average-sized boy, and Zachary, a little person.

The doctors were thrilled that Amy was able to hold on for thirty-four weeks. That is a remarkable length of time for a dwarf woman to carry twins. Nevertheless, they were still technically premature. They had to stay in the hospital longer than normal: about two and a half weeks. That was fine with us because it allowed Amy to better recover from cesarean section birth of twins. She needed all the rest she could get before taking on the everyday rigors of caring for two infants.

We were beginning a new adventure in our lives together: parenthood.

PARENTHOOD AS A LITTLE PERSON

I have been blessed in a great many ways; so many, in fact, that it is hard to list them all. I have parents who've made what could have been an impossibly difficult childhood into a positive memory. I have lasting friendships. I have a great career, and I've enjoyed unusual success in my chosen line of work. And I thank God for a beautiful, loving wife.

But there is a blessing that stands apart from the rest. It's a blessing that fulfills me in so many ways, challenges me in even more, and gives me a deep sense of responsibility, purpose, and being needed. I'm talking about one of the greatest gifts of married life: fatherhood.

Like my parents' kids—Ruth, Matthew, Joshua, and Samuel—all of my kids have biblical names: Jeremy (Jeremiah), Zachary (Zachariah), Jacob, and Molly (okay, so Molly as a derivative of Mary is a stretch). Zachary is our only little person. We always say that we are the perfectly balanced family—Molly might argue that point because she's the only girl among four children—because we have three little people and three average-sized people.

To our knowledge, we're the only little people parents who have four natural kids. We know of several dwarf couples with two children, a few with three, and some blended families with four or more, but no others with four natural kids. A dwarf couple having twins is rare, but being a couple with four children may be unique.

After Molly (our third child) was born, we had decided to call it quits as far as having children was concerned. But God had other plans, and he sent us another gift in the form of our youngest son, Jacob. God works out his designs without consulting us. Imagine that.

When Amy was pregnant with Jacob, our three kids had their own preferences for their new sibling. Molly wanted a little sister and Jeremy wanted a brother. Zachary wanted a little brother also, but he hoped our last child would be a little person so he could have a brother who was just like him. "Mom, I'd like to have a little person like me for a brother," he said. Of course he had little people in Mom and Dad, but sometimes Mom and Dad don't cut it for a kid his age.

Jacob wasn't born a little person. That was great with everyone in the family—including Zachary.

As a parent, it is a joy and a wonder to watch your children grow—physically, emotionally, and spiritually—and see the differences between them. Sometimes when I'm with my kids, I wonder how each of them, with the same two parents, could be developing personality traits that are so different from one another's. Each of our children is unique. Jeremy, Zachary, Molly, and Jacob are alike in many ways, yet completely different in others. I can already see the talents, skills, and personality traits that will lead them in different paths as they grow.

It amazes me sometimes the depth of love I feel for my children. I'd always been told the love of a parent is something you can't fully comprehend until you have children yourself. Now that I'm a father, I understand. I love my kids more than life itself. There is nothing I wouldn't do to care for them, protect them, and make sure they are comfortable.

My family isn't perfect. Like any family, we have conflicts, times where we are down, times where we need every bit of patience to continue to function successfully as a family. But I take great joy in seeing how I, my wife, and my children grow together in a loving family environment.

Being a father isn't an easy calling. I remember when Jeremy and Zachary were only three years old. We'd been riding around the farm on our ATV. We decided to explore an area off our farm, down a draw, through a thicket, and across a field to a creek. As I attempted to cross the creek, the ATV got stuck in the mud. I was unable to free it even with my two boys pushing with all their might. I didn't have my crutches and felt a little trapped. I decided this would be a good opportunity for the boys to learn the confidence that comes from succeeding through a difficult situation.

"Jeremy, do you think you can find your way back to the house?" I asked. It was close to a mile and through an area he'd never been before.

"I think so," came the uncertain response. His tone implied he was both concerned and excited about the challenge.

"Great. You'll be a real hero if you can find your way back and have Mom bring the Jeep and a big chain."

I must say I was a little nervous as Jeremy headed up the hill toward our farm. A lot can happen to a three-year-old, but I knew we were surrounded by many farmhouses, and if he did get offtrack, he would easily be found by some farmer plowing his field. I figured it was much more likely he would find the house, and his confidence would be bolstered from the mission.

It wasn't more than an hour later that Amy came driving over that hill with Jeremy in the front seat pointing her directions the whole way.

Parenthood is full of all sorts of challenges, many of which I probably haven't even thought about yet. Each day as a parent has a new set of problems and victories, questions and answers. I've made plenty of mistakes as a father, but I'm grateful I've been able to adapt to being a daddy.

There's something both frightening and thrilling about knowing I am responsible for shaping these four young people's lives. But I wouldn't trade fatherhood for anything in the world: it's just the kind of challenge I love to meet head on.

TEACHING THE ACCEPTABLE

One of the special challenges Amy and I face as two little people with four children is helping them understand and properly respond to the differences between our family and those of their friends.

What makes it a challenge is the fact that our children know no other life. To them, this is what a family is like. One time another little girl asked Molly what was wrong with Amy. Her answer was quoted in the newspaper: "Are you crazy? She's a little mom! Can't you see that?" Our kids don't understand how rare a family like ours is. They have no clue that other people don't see our family from the same perspective they do.

Amy and I try to make sure our children understand what is and isn't acceptable behavior in a social situation. When we are shopping, we expect them to behave, to keep the noise down to an acceptable level, and to stay close to us. We want them to know they will see people doing unacceptable things out in the world, but that there is a proper way to talk and behave.

We also want them to know there are acceptable ways to respond to people who react poorly when they see these two little people and their four children. We try to teach them that in the real world, people won't always say and do what is politically correct, that sometimes people will say and do insensitive—even offensive—things. They need to understand that sometimes such things are said because little people look different, sometimes the comments are out of ignorance, and unfortunately, sometimes things are said out of cruelty.

When they hear children say, "That mom and dad are little," or use terms such as "dwarf" or "midget," we want them to understand that not everybody knows what it's like to be a little person or to have a little person for a mom or dad. Not all people know how to respond when they see a little person. We want them to understand that lots of kids their age may not even know what a dwarf is or even that there is such a thing.

We want our children to respond wisely when they see or hear something they know isn't right. For example, we want Jeremy to feel loyalty to Zachary and to stand up for him if someone mistreats him. But we want him to do it in the right way. We want Jeremy—as well as Zachary, Molly, and Jacob—to know how to handle it appropriately when people say or do inappropriate things.

I want my children to grow up with respect and compassion for people who are different from them—people with handicaps or disabilities, people who talk differently than they do, people of different ethnicity. These attitudes start at home because my kids are being raised by two little people, including a dad who hobbles around on crutches or uses a cart to get around in places like shopping malls or grocery stores.

My kids will also respect those different from themselves because they are growing up with a little person. Having Zachary gives Amy and me ample opportunity to encourage the children to think about what it's like to be little and how they can help make somebody who's different feel comfortable.

Jeremy and Zachary, because they are twins, have a special bond, a closeness that goes beyond that of most brothers. They do a lot of the same things for fun, and they have a lot of the same friends. When they have friends over, they run all around the farm playing in the orchards, in the barn, in the mine shaft, and in the tree house.

Zachary does his best to keep up with the other boys, but sometimes his short legs have a hard time keeping pace, and he's come in the house crying to Amy and me that his brother is leaving him in the dust. This presents a great opportunity for us to teach both boys something. On the one hand, we don't want Zachary blaming his brother when he falls behind, and we tell him to ask Jeremy to wait for him to catch up once in a while. On Jeremy's side, when we can catch him apart from his "little" brother, we talk to him about showing some sensitivity to Zachary. We remind him that the kids who come over to visit are Zach's friends, too, and he needs to think about his brother when they're out playing.

SOME EMPATHY FOR OUR BOY

As great a job as Amy's parents and my parents did raising us and getting us through the tough times that our smallness brought, there is an advantage Amy and I have in raising Zachary that they didn't have: We know what it is like to be little in an average-sized world.

As compassionate and loving as my parents were with me, as great as they were at raising me and my brothers with all our physical problems, they will never know what it's like to *be* a little person. There was a limit to their understanding, simply because they've never seen the world through the eyes of someone who would never grow much taller than four feet.

Zachary knows he's different than his brothers and sister, his friends, and the other kids in his school. He knows he's like his mom and dad, and he understands that there are other little people in the world other than himself and his parents. We are honest with Zachary about those differences. We don't sugarcoat things for him. Without scaring him into a shell, we try to let him know that life as a little person will be tough at times. But we also try to let him know that he can make it, that he can have a good life as a little person, just like Mom and Dad have.

We teach Zachary that his self-confidence has to come from within because it's not going to come from the world around him. We teach him that the self-confidence he has should stem from the fact that he is made by God, and God doesn't make mistakes. We teach him he is a valuable person who has much to offer and that there is nothing "wrong" with him, only that he is different from most people around him.

We also teach Zachary to go beyond surviving, to use his skills and talents to thrive. That is the way I was raised, and that's the way I am raising all my kids. I believe any parent, particularly a parent of a little person or a child with a disability, should raise his or her children this way. I believe raising kids with an eye on survival and not on excelling at whatever they do teaches them to aim low and never to aspire to anything more than the bare minimum.

While we show understanding and compassion to Zachary because of his difference from other kids, we don't coddle him. That isn't the way either of us was raised. My parents had to go to extraordinary lengths to get me through my early childhood, but they never allowed me to feel sorry for myself or expect that other people would cater to me because I was little.

Amy's parents were the same way. They treated her the same way they treated her siblings. If the phone on the wall was too high for her to reach, she would have to get a stool if she wanted to use it. If she couldn't see over the counter when she was baking cookies, she needed to find a chair. Amy's parents' attitude was that she had to adapt to a world that wasn't made for her because it wasn't, for the most part, going to adapt to her.

It might sound like "tough love," and in some respects I guess it is. But those types of lessons are better—and more comfortably—learned in the home, where there is a safe, loving environment. It is in this environment that we are teaching Zachary how to adapt to the world using his mind. We teach him not to be overbearing or bossy, just to stand up for himself in an appropriate way and not allow himself to be underestimated because he's small.

A TOUGH START

Zachary was a good-natured baby, happy and smiling most of the time. But he was sick a lot. He would get violently ill, vomiting with no warning at least three or four times a week. That wasn't his only problem. We couldn't always put a finger on what was wrong, but there was something that was just off about this little boy. He wasn't growing or progressing physically the way he should have, and he had several episodes that required attention, the most memorable—and terrifying—of them in February of 1991, when he was nine months old.

My mother and father were visiting from California, and, as usual, they were having a ball spending time with the grandchildren. Then, with no warning, Zachary let out a sickening little whimper, collapsed, and stopped breathing. One second he was laughing and playing with his grandmother, the next he was limp as a rag doll.

There was no question about it: my son was dying. He looked dead already. His eyes were fixed, he was limp, and his skin was a horrible shade of blue. I wondered if it was time for him to go. He'd been sick a lot, and the thought occurred to me that this at least would be the end of his struggles.

As I dialed 911, I remember thinking how far in the country we lived, how it would take a while for any medical help to arrive. As the dispatcher said, "Nine-one-one," I tried desperately to remain calm and tell him the facts. "I have a nine-month-old male with achondroplasia dwarfism who's NOT BREATHING!"

"Where is he now?" the dispatcher asked.

"He's with my mother."

"Okay, lay him down on the floor."

I relayed to my mom, "Lay him down!"

The dispatcher calmly said, "Put a finger in his mouth and clear any obstruction in his airway."

"Maybe we should throw him in the car and head for the hospital!" I said.

"Do you want to talk," the dispatcher said, "or listen?"

"I want to listen."

"Tell your mother to place her mouth over the baby's and breathe three short breaths."

"Mom, three short breaths into Zach."

My mother calmly started mouth-to-mouth resuscitation. She'd done this several times before with Josh.

Just then I heard Zachary start to sputter and breathe. "He's breathing!" I screamed. "He's breathing!" In a few minutes, the ambulance arrived to take him to the hospital.

Zachary stayed in the hospital for about ten days, as the doctors treated him for what turned out to be a respiratory virus, a condition that would have been like a bad cold for his twin brother but which for him nearly meant an early death.

That was the low point in Zachary's early childhood, but he had several other episodes. We knew something was wrong with Zachary. He couldn't lift his head without extraordinary effort, and he just wasn't progressing the way he should have. We took him to several doctors, and no one could tell us what was wrong. Most of the doctors just told us to give him some time, that he would "grow out of it."

Zachary was not quite two years old when, in a last-minute move, we took him to the 1991 LPA national convention in Dallas, where we knew there would be doctors who specialized in the physical problems of achondroplastic children. Among those was Dr. Charles Scott, who is on the medical advisory board affiliated with the LPA and a specialist in achondroplasia.

We got in to see Dr. Scott, and he recognized immediately that something was seriously wrong. "He's not right," he said. "He's got a serious problem." One condition Dr. Scott suggested was a common problem with achondroplastic children: compression of the brain stem resulting from the opening of the skull at the top of the spinal column, known as the *foramen magnum*, being too small to accommodate the spinal cord. It seemed like an accurate diagnosis because Zachary suffered all the symptoms of that condition.

From Dallas, we flew Zachary to Baltimore's Johns Hopkins University Medical School, where he was examined by doctors who specialized in the physical problems of little people. It was there that we found Zachary's problem was a condition called hydrocephalus, meaning he had excess fluid on his brain because the drainage openings in his skull were too small. We found out that all people with achondroplasia have hydrocephalus to some extent, but that most of them suffer no ill effects from the condition. In Zachary's case, it was a serious problem, and he had a shunt, a device that aids in drainage of fluids, surgically implanted in the base of his spine.

It was nerve-wracking for Amy and me when Zachary went in for surgery. I wanted to make sure he was in the hands of doctors who knew how to handle the special problems of little people. I know too many horror stories about little people who have been treated by doctors who didn't know the differences. Too many doctors believe the procedures are always the same, that people are people. But there are differences, and I wanted to make certain the doctors who worked on my son—or me or Amy—knew what they were.

HOW WILL WE DO IT?

Amy and I wonder sometimes how we will handle the situations sure to come our way simply because we are the parents of four children. We've already gone through some trying situations with our children—including our son's near death—and we've come through it successfully. But we know it is just the beginning. We still have close to two decades of child rearing to get through.

I wonder how I will handle it when my beautiful daughter Molly becomes a young woman, when young boys—some (most?) of whom my fatherly instincts will make me dislike from the moment I see them—start showing interest in her. I wonder how Amy will respond if her youngest son, this wide-shouldered, thick-chested boy, announces he wants to play a dangerous game like football. How will we handle the heartbreaks of lost love that are so much a part of teenagers' lives? How will we respond to the report cards that indicate that better effort is needed? What will we say to our sons when they come home telling us that they have gotten into those oh-so-typical boyhood scraps? How will we handle it when Zachary comes home hurt by what someone has said?

We just will. Like any Mom and Dad, Amy and I will continue to grow into the job of being parents. We'll make our share of mistakes, lose a few battles, and feel completely inadequate at times. But I know we'll succeed, and we'll love every minute of it.

LIVING IN A TALL MAN'S WORLD

Billy Barty, the founder and former president of Little People of America, said, "You don't know discrimination until you walk up to a nineteen-inch-high urinal with your thirteen-inch inseam."

While I'm sure those who design and build public restroom facilities have no feelings of ill will toward little people, Billy's anecdote is still a good example of the kinds of problems we little people face in the everyday world. The world just can't make every adjustment to make life easier on me.

The 1990 Americans with Disabilities Act, which was aimed at making aspects of American society more accessible to people with disabilities, together with other improvements, have helped make life easier for people with handicaps—including little people. But there is only so much the world can do to accommodate me and other disabled people.

The rest, I have learned, is up to me.

BEING LITTLE CHANGES THINGS

In the 1985 shoot-'em-up Western *Silverado*, Paden, a drifter played by Kevin Kline, observes that a diminutive but feisty barmaid by the name of Stella (played by Linda Hunt) is standing behind the bar on a ramp she has had constructed for herself to allow her to serve customers at her saloon on an eye-to-eye basis. Paden is impressed with Stella's ingenuity, and he's even more struck when she tells him, "The world is what you make of it, my friend. If it doesn't fit, you make alterations."

As a little person living in a tall person's world, I know how true Stella's words are. We little people live in a world that presents problems most people wouldn't even consider. I'm talking about things most people take absolutely for granted, the most everyday things you could think of—or not think of, until they become inconveniences.

I've learned to make alterations in my own little world, some of them relatively minor but others that are absolutely vital for me to make it in this world. Some of the alterations are of the physical world around me, while others are alterations of how I choose to do things.

One silly example of that I often cite is how I drink my coffee. Anyone who knows me knows I like my coffee. I drink it at home, on the road, in airplanes, at business meetings. I drink my coffee black. Not too long ago it occurred to me why. It's because it is difficult for me to reach the cream and sugar at a coffee shop. Think about it. Next time you go to your local Starbuck's, look at where the cream and sugar are. I can't even *see* the cream and sugar at most coffee shops, let alone reach it. I've come to prefer my coffee black, but I have wondered if I might have been a cream and sugar guy if I'd been taller, or if the cream and sugar had been placed lower.

When it came to coffee drinking, I almost unconsciously made an adjustment to the world around me. But there are other things that require more thought and effort in order to adjust to them, day-to-day things that are the absolute necessities of life.

Think for a moment about how difficult it would be for someone who is four feet tall to use public accommodations—such as restrooms—that are designed for average-sized people, or to use pay phones or automated teller machines when you can't see the keypads, or to order from a fast-food restaurant when the counters are nose high, or to shop in grocery stores in which half the merchandise is placed on shelves too high to reach.

Think about the problems presented by living in a home where the countertops are too high. The shower nozzle is set for someone over five feet tall. You can't see out the windows. The clothing rods in the closets are unreachable, and you have a difficult time negotiating the stairs because the risers are built for someone with average-length legs.

What about working for a company whose entire facility is made to accommodate people who are at least five feet tall, whose offices don't fit someone your height? Think for just a moment how being little affects things like driving, riding on a public transit system, going to the movies, going for rides at the amusement park ("You must be taller than this sign to go on this ride"), or walking around safely in a crowded parking lot.

Those are the kinds of problems little people deal with every day. Some are minor inconveniences, while others can be major burdens. Some things can be adjusted for us, while others are things to which we need to adjust. For example, our family vehicles are equipped with specially-designed brake and gas pedal extensions that allow Amy and me to drive them without making it impossible for an average-sized person to drive them.

Clothing for little people is always a problem. Unless you are rich enough to have all your clothes specially made for you, alterations—sometimes extensive ones—are a must if you want your clothes to fit properly. It is not possible for most little people to buy clothes that are ready to wear off the rack. While some can wear children's sizes, most of us have to buy adult sizes and have them altered. For example, I can buy Levi's blue jeans that fit me around the waist, but the inseams aren't even close. I can buy regular-sized men's shirts that fit well in the shoulders and chest, but the arms are too long. Fortunately for me, my wife knows how to do alterations.

When we remodeled our house, we made very few accommodations for ourselves. There are some differences, but most people wouldn't even notice. For example, the stair risers aren't as high as normal ones, and the windows are placed so we can see out without having to use a chair. The kitchen is by and large the same as any other, and Amy has learned to use stools, chairs, and drawers—pulled out all the way at the bottom, then less and less on each succeeding drawer, so as to make a makeshift set of stairs—to reach the things she needs.

We decided early not to make too many accommodations on the house because we realized that one day we might want to sell. A house altered for little people may have reduced market value simply because a buyer would know up front that he'd have to spend some money to remodel. It's also fortunate that we didn't alter the house because we have three averaged-sized kids living there, as well as countless average-sized adults visiting every year. Amy and I are going to build another home on our property, and we plan to make some special accommodations for ourselves then.

STARES, QUESTIONS, AND COMMENTS

Relating to people as a little person can be a challenge on several levels (no pun intended), one of which is that of greeting people. I want to be able to walk up to someone, look him in the eye, and shake hands, man to man. But to do that, an average-sized person has to stoop down.

There are more serious issues we little people have to address in our relationships, both in private and in public. Among the most serious is how I respond to the way people—adults and children alike—react when they first see me.

I hadn't been around very long until I realized something: I look different. I draw attention. Whenever I'm out in public—in church, at the grocery store, at restaurants—people stare. What they see is so different from what they are used to they have to take a second or third look. As hard as they may try not to look, thinking it's impolite, they look anyway.

I've gotten used to it over the years, and I think I've developed a healthy approach to it. I also got some help learning how to handle the curious from my father. Dad used to tell me, "When people stare at you, take it as a compliment. They stare because you're unique and worth evaluating. They are taking some of their precious time to check you out, and it's not derogatory. They just want to know about you."

Dad learned that wisdom the hard way. He remembers how he'd feel aggravated—even angry—when people would stare at Sam and me. He still talks about how he was ready to confront people he caught staring at us to let them know we were real children with real feelings and not some kind of sideshow.

Eventually, Dad realized people were going to stare because of the uniqueness of our family. He thought about his attitudes, prayed for wisdom, and came to the conclusion that it wasn't worth the energy it took to get angry because people looked at us. Instead, he decided to take those opportunities to help people understand why my brother and I looked the way we did and what it was like to live with that condition.

NO OFFENSE, BUT...

I'm not easy to offend. In fact, I can't remember the last time as an adult when I was offended by something someone said about me individually or about little people in general. I sometimes get a kick out of talking to people who aren't familiar with dwarfism or who are worried about saying the wrong thing. I try to put people at ease by letting them know there is little they could say—outside of an intentional personal insult—that would offend me.

I don't take offense when someone calls me a midget. I used to call my little brother Sam "midge." I wanted us both to get used to hearing it. To this day, if someone calls me a midget, I don't feel the slightest sting, and I'll bet Sam doesn't either. That doesn't mean all little people feel this way. It's a hurtful word for many of us.

Terms such as *short-statured, little people,* and *dwarf* are all considered acceptable. Little people refer to non-dwarfs as "average-sized"—even those who are very tall—rather than "normal" because, as Billy Barty has been saying for years, "I have never found anybody who is normal."

I'm also not offended by the things other little people do to make a living. For example, I recently heard a story about a middle-aged little person working in a Mexican restaurant in Texas. His job was to walk amongst the tables wearing a sombrero with chips and salsa on the brim. The customers would take the chips and salsa and leave him a tip. It was a silly thing for the guy to do, but it was a living, and I respect the fact that he was at least working. A high-ranking member of Little People of America appeared on a television news show and expressed his outrage that this man would do that. His logic was that little people need to stick to more "dignified" ways to make money. (Perhaps someone should point out to him that average-sized people do some pretty stupid things for money, too.)

That's a good example of a time when we should leave well enough alone. If someone wants to make a living doing something we consider silly or stupid, that's his business. I don't care if it's dwarf tossing, dwarf bowling, or appearing in sideshows. To me, if there's nothing inherently immoral or illegal about what they are doing, we should leave them alone. I believe that when a little person— particularly one who is high up in our association—makes an issue of things other little people do, it creates a climate of hypersensitivity, a climate in which average-sized people are afraid to talk to us or ask us questions for fear of saying something that will offend.

One of the reasons I'm not easy to offend is I realize there is such a lack of understanding or knowledge about little people in our culture. I don't believe we should get angry or offended when someone says something out of ignorance. There is a big difference between saying something out of ignorance and using names like "runt" or "shrimp" in order to hurt.

It amuses me how the same people who try so hard to be politically correct or "sensitive," the ones who fancy themselves the most enlightened, are often the ones most likely to say something inappropriate or to discriminate. They always use the right terminology, but there is something in their attitude that reeks of pity when pity is the last thing little people want.

A HEART FOR THE KIDS

I've always found I'm most comfortable around people who say what they are thinking and ask the questions the "politically correct" don't have the nerve to ask. It's especially that way with children. They are the most uneducated, unenlightened, and unrefined among us, yet I have the best times interacting with them in a public setting, simply because there is such a lack of malice in the questions they ask.

When children stare, it's because they see someone who looks so different from anyone they've ever seen before. When they ask me why I'm shorter than they are—even though they're only ten—or why I drag my leg behind me when I walk, or why my arms are so short for my size, or why my hands look so funny, they do so only because they are curious. I see it as a chance to help them learn there are people in the world who are very different from themselves, yet the same in so many ways.

Sometimes when Amy and I go shopping, I position myself in the aisle at the store so kids will see me. When they look wide eyed at me, I love to start chatting with them so they see I'm just like anyone else. "Have you ever seen anyone like me before?" I'll ask them. Or I'll say, "Have you ever used crutches before?"

I was walking through a store recently when a boy about ten years old turned the corner, saw me, and looked at me in wide-eyed curiosity. I could see in his eyes that he'd never seen anyone like me before. Here I was, shorter than he was, yet he could see I was an adult. I caught his eye, smiled at him, and gave him a friendly, "How you doing, partner?" He smiled back at me and said, "Fine!" then followed his father down the next aisle. I chuckled to myself and thought, *Mission accomplished!*

While I like talking to the kids, I often find myself laughing inside at the horrified looks on the parents' faces when a child asks me a question. I detest it when parents react angrily when their kids stare or ask direct questions. When that happens, I just want to tell the parent, "Doggone it! That's how kids are. When someone is different, they stare. I can handle it."

WORKING WITHIN THE SYSTEM

Whether they verbalize it or not, people naturally equate tallness with competence, confidence, and intelligence. If you add a little handsomeness to the equation, that person has the world by the tail. There is just something about a tall, good-looking person walking into a room that gets people's attention.

I know from personal experience that if a tall person and a little person walk into, say, an automobile showroom, the tall person will be approached by the salesman first, at least nine times out of ten. There is the assumption that because the person is tall, he is more likely to be able to afford a new car.

In the corporate world, taller people are far more likely to be hired, then advanced and promoted to upper-level management, than little people. It's discriminatory, to be sure, if only on a subconscious level, but it happens all the time. I've known many little people who have been discriminated against—often in a way they can't prove. One of those was my wife.

In college, Amy majored in personnel management and hospitality, which is for hotel and restaurant management—a very appearance-oriented line of work. Amy loves to prepare and serve food, and she wanted to make a living doing that. One of the requirements for graduation in that major is to serve an internship. She was told she had an internship at a hotel, but after meeting with the manager, she was declined for it. She was never told, but Amy knew it was because she was a dwarf. She was as talented as any of the other internship candidates, but her appearance kept her from getting it.

There's no question there is an advantage in our culture, and in our business world, to being tall. On the other hand, I've found there are huge advantages to being little—if you know how to work within the system.

I am grateful to live in a place like America where there is, by and large, acceptance and understanding for disabled people. I think our culture has done much to make our lives easier and more enjoyable, and improvements are still being made all the time.

I don't believe in being demanding or pushy simply because I am disabled, and I've never taken an attitude that anything is owed me. I would never file a lawsuit over something like not being able to reach items on the upper shelves of grocery stores or slipping and falling on a wet driveway. I understand that the rest of the world, while it can do some things to make my life easier, can't always accommodate my needs. I understand that walking around on crutches in itself presents certain risks I have to take if I'm to venture outside my home.

Yes, there are some advantages afforded disabled people, but I hesitate to call them advantages. They are simply means of leveling the playing field and allowing people like me to take an active part in society.

To me, the real advantages of being little come from learning how to use people's responses and reactions to your advantage. I learned very early there is something almost magical about the way people respond to me as a little person, and I have learned to use that magic to my advantage.

RESPONDING TO LOWERED EXPECTATIONS

Amy and I understand it strikes people as almost surreal when they see two little people with four kids. It's not something you see every day. Just seeing a little person is unusual enough, but seeing two parents, each around four feet tall—including the dad riding a cart—with their four children is, to most people, otherworldly.

Amy has heard several comments from children. One little girl, looking wide eyed at Amy and the kids in a shopping mall, said out loud to her mother, "Mom, she's a little mom." That was followed with a horrified, embarrassed, "Don't say that! Come on," as the innocent little child's mother hurried her away. But Amy wasn't offended. She *is* a "little mom."

It's usually the adults that bother Amy. She's been known to get a little miffed at people who seem to have a hard time believing the four kids she has with her are hers. One woman actually approached her in public and asked in most surprised tones if they were her kids. When Amy told her they were, she said, "Oh my goodness! How can you do it!"

The assumption most people make is that if a dwarf has children, the children will be dwarfs. She and I, as well as most little people, understand the American public in general knows little to nothing about dwarfs. What bothers her, though, is that there is an underlying assumption that because she is little, she somehow can't handle being a mother the way an average-sized woman can.

Being a mother is very important to Amy. She can't stand the thought of allowing her littleness to cause her to fail at anything, especially at being a mom. I think Amy is a clear candidate for Mother of the Decade. And anybody who knows her would tell you the same thing.

But Amy has always said her greatest fear is that someone would come and take her children away because they didn't believe she was capable of caring for them properly. That has never come close to happening—and there's no reason to believe it ever will—but the thought haunts her.

I love to surpass the lowered expectations people place on me because I'm small. I don't care what anyone tells me, when a group of suits at a business meeting sees a dwarf show up, their expectations go through the floor. It takes very little to exceed those kinds of expectations, and when I do, I have them right where I want them.

When I go out on a sales call, my company often won't tell the prospective buyer that I'm a little person. I love walking into the room and seeing the looks on people's faces when they see me. I can just see the words *Nobody told us!* tattooed on their foreheads as they see me—all four feet, two inches of me—carrying myself into their meeting on crutches.

I also learned early I can get away with things an average-sized person cannot. There's no question in my mind that I can use my appearance to my advantage, simply because people tend to be a little more tolerant of me because I'm little. In fact, I think some of my personality traits would be downright obnoxious if I were tall, but somehow they work because I'm little.

My mother always told me I needed to dress sharper and look good because of my disability. On the whole, I think that's true, and I try to present myself well when I go on sales calls. I try to dress nicely, keep my shirt tucked in, and in general look professional. On the other hand, I have learned I can get away with little things like a coffee stain on my shirt. Where someone else might be embarrassed, I just look at the stain, hold up my hands—those gnarled hands with the stumpy fingers that struggle just to grip a pen—and say, "My dexterity isn't so good this morning."

I use a little self-effacing humor to put people at ease because I know people are not only surprised to see me, they also can be a little uncomfortable. It's my way of letting them know that I'm here, I belong here, and I feel like I fit in here.

JUST FITTING IN

When I was in junior high school, I had a good friend I felt sorry for. I'll call him Bill. Bill was a handsome guy—blond-haired, blue-eyed, and muscular—but he was shorter than most of the boys. One day, I came home from school and told my dad I felt sorry for him because he was short. It didn't matter to me that Bill was almost a foot taller than I was; I felt bad for him because he was shorter than most of his friends and classmates.

"I feel so sorry for Bill," I said.

"Why?" my dad asked.

"Because he's so short," I answered.

Dad couldn't contain his amusement. With a look on his face that was both incredulous and amused, he said to me, "You're feeling sorry for Bill because he's short?"

"Yes." I said, with conviction.

"You're short, too!" Dad pointed out.

"Yeah, but I have a reason for being short."

My father tells people that this exchange confirmed to him I didn't mind being little, that I felt I did fit in.

There aren't many people around who don't in some way wonder if they fit in. There is always something that sets people apart, be it height, skin color, the way they talk, their social or economic status, their family backgrounds, or some physical handicap. Sadly, many little people—as well as others with even more serious disabilities—allow those things to keep them from living productive, active lives.

I was brought up in a family environment that bred self-confidence, an attitude that my short stature didn't have to keep me from doing the things I wanted to do. There was an emphasis placed on love for one another, love for God, and confidence in the fact that he had a plan. This was the biggest advantage I had in overcoming my disabilities. I had a sense of belonging, a sense that I had something to offer.

But I understand not all little people—or other people with disabilities—have that advantage. Many little people have no idea what it takes to get where they want to go in life or how to get what they need from the world around them. In other words, they don't feel like they fit in anywhere.

Those feelings of detachment have had some tragic results in the lives of many people with disabilities. Some, with a cloud of despair hanging over their heads because they don't feel they belong, choose the prison of alcohol or drug abuse. Others I've known have chosen suicide as a way out of their despair.

If there is one thing I want people to take from this book it is this: You can fit in and you can contribute something to this world. You can make a difference in other people's lives. You can make your corner of the world a better place to live.

REACHING BEYOND THE MINIMUM

I've always believed life is a lot like a farmer's field: you get out of it what you put into it. I believe I've done more than survive in a world not tailored for me because I have never been the kind of person who does just enough to get by. I've always believed in making the most of the talents and gifts I have, whether it concerns my mind, body, finances, or anything else. I'm not talking about overcompensating, but about simply being a good steward of the talents and gifts God has given us.

Case in point: my farm.

NOT YOUR ORDINARY FARM

When I first bought my farm, I didn't think of just making it a nice piece of land with a farmhouse, a barn, and a white fence around it. I wanted to go the extra mile with it, do some things a lot of people thought were crazy. I had visions of things for the kids like a paved tricycle track. Later, those dreams evolved to include a three-level tree house, a replica of a pirate ship on the irrigation pond, a movable "Old West" town complete with a complex of underground tunnels, and a mine shaft that runs under the newly-restored barn.

I'm not finished, either. I'm working on the Tower of Terror. It's an upright tower about twenty-four feet tall that shakes and sways at the top. It's going to be completely safe but scary at the same time—like my own personal carnival ride. The idea for the Tower of Terror came to me simply because I am scared of high places, and a safe, enclosed structure that is high and moves sounds like my idea of a thrill ride.

I haven't created the things on this farm for any kind of business purpose or to make money. The farm is something of a novelty, but it's also our private home, and—for now, at least—we want to keep it that way.

The only real business aspects of the farm are the peach orchards and blueberry fields. We open up the farm for a few weeks in the summer for the U-pick season. We get picked out almost as soon as we put up the signs announcing the fruit is ripe. We've thought about canning specialty jams—something Amy is quite talented at—to sell during the U-pick season, and I've looked into buying some industrial canning equipment.

The orchard is more of a hobby than a business since the money we make selling the fruit just covers the cost of the sprays and other expenses in having an orchard. I've had offers to sell my peaches commercially, but we plan to keep our farm a U-pick operation because we like having people visit.

WHY BOTHER?

With everything I have going on in my professional life, I'm often asked why I make things all the harder on myself by taking on all these projects on the farm. Why do I bother with things like a tree house, a pirate ship, an old barn, or an Old West town? All that on top of a full-time job and a good-sized peach orchard.

I've gone beyond the minimums with the farm because it is challenging and fun. I've enjoyed making it unique, something my children can enjoy. The farm is a "happening" place for my kids and their friends. Jeremy and Zachary have friends over almost every day, so at any given time you can find a pack of boys here playing on the boat, in the mine shaft, or in the Old West town. The farm is also a great place for adults to meet. We have an annual Roloff Farms Picnic, where we invite hundreds of friends and coworkers. The farm is also the site of lots of church-related activities, such as picnics.

More than that, though, I love to dream up things that, on the surface, appear difficult—maybe even impossible—then work on ways to make those dreams reality. Whether it's a programming problem, or a marketing problem, or something I want to accomplish on the farm for my kids, I like to look at what I want to accomplish, then create a solution or adapt an existing solution. There is just something inside me that likes to solve problems, and I get satisfaction in seeing the solutions pay dividends.

From the time I was a little kid, I was never one to set my sights on the bare minimum, on survival. If I were, I could easily work my eight-to-five job, go home, have dinner with the wife and kids, then plop down in front of the TV for the rest of the evening. But I believe our time and other resources here on this earth are limited, and we can choose one of two ways to use that time: waste it or make good use of it.

"Just getting by" isn't the way I was brought up. That wouldn't have worked in a family like ours. I can think of one year in the life of the Roloff family that pounded that point home for life. It was a year none of us will ever forget, a year in which we learned the value of going the extra step.

AN INCREDIBLE YEAR

The Christmas season of 1974 was an incredible one for the Roloff family. It was a year in which we all—Mom and Dad, Ruth, me, Joshua, and Sam— began what would be one of the most difficult yet exciting times of our lives together as a family. It was a year in which Mom and Dad were stretched to almost breaking, a year in which Sam and I endured incredible physical pain, and a year in which Joshua by all accounts *should* have died. It was a year in which both Mom and Dad, in addition to all they endured with us kids, both had relatives die.

It's not an understatement to say that Christmas of 1974 marked the start of a period of suffering in our family. It was the start of a year that many families might not have survived. But mine did, and each one of us underwent incredible personal and spiritual growth. It was a year that in many ways defined what my family is all about.

Sam and I were both away from our family that year, staying at the Shriners Hospital in San Francisco. I had undergone some of the more painful procedures I would ever endure. That was a difficult time for the Roloff family, but as difficult as those times were, things were going to get decidedly tougher in the months ahead.

During the days before and after Christmas, Joshua (then ten-years-old) started having severe headaches. He'd already survived several brushes with death because of his heart and lung conditions, and had gone through open-heart surgery the previous fall. These were searing headaches that caused his vision to blur. They were the symptom of a terrible medical condition.

On January 6, Joshua lapsed into a coma and had to be rushed in for life-saving emergency brain surgery to remove an abscess. The doctors who worked on Josh didn't know if he would even survive the surgery.

Around the time of Josh's brain surgery, my father came to the Shriners Hospital to get Sam and me. Ordinarily, Shriners wouldn't allow a patient to leave early. Once you checked in, you stayed until they said you could go. But Dad wasn't taking no for an answer. At first the hospital administrators resisted Dad's request, but he was adamant: "Look, these boys' brother is dying, and he needs them there with him. They have to go with me, and they have to go now!"

We needed to be in the hospital, but Joshua needed us with him even more. This was a dire emergency, and Dad let it be known that we *were* going to be leaving with him that day. We packed what few things we had brought with us to the hospital, and we left with Dad. To our knowledge, that was the first time Shriners ever prematurely discharged a patient from the hospital.

Sam and I had no idea our brother had undergone emergency brain surgery when we left Shriners Hospital and went to Stanford Hospital with Dad that day. We didn't know he was near death. We only knew what little Dad had explained to us: Josh was sick and needed us with him. We also had no idea we were about to start seven weeks of touch-and-go time for Josh, seven weeks during which we spent most of our waking hours in the hospital, either visiting with him or waiting for him to come to consciousness.

During that whole time, Dad seldom if ever slept in his bed or had a chance to go home for some rest. He'd get off work after a ten- to twelve-hour night shift, head straight for the hospital, visit with us and Mom and Josh, then catch a nap on the bench outside the hospital room, his only "luxuries" a change of clothes and some toiletries to wash up with. After his forty-wink respite, he was out the door again to work another shift. To this day, I wonder how he did it.

Joshua survived the operation for the brain abscess, but again had to go into heart surgery at Stanford University on May 31. Later, Mom's uncle died and two of my young cousins—my father's brother's twins, who were about a year old—drowned in the family swimming pool. All the while, Sam and I were enduring our own physical problems. We were both in body casts at the start of the year, and after I got out of the cast, I had to spend most of the rest of the year sitting in a cushion that looked like a ring filled with Jell-O.

Every week it seemed like there was some new crisis to manage. But in the midst of all that craziness, our lives went on. We had birthdays (Ruth turned thirteen that year) and family outings. We handled the normal day-to-day issues of family life. We loved one another, argued with one another, forgave one another. We continued to go to church and, as much as possible, school. We still had our friends come visit us. Dad continued to work his job, and Mom kept the home running as smoothly as possible.

And, as if the burdens weren't already enough to bear, as if they didn't have enough concerns just taking care of their own kids, Mom and Dad willingly and joyfully took on some additional responsibilities.

INCREASING THE LOAD…GLADLY

The second half of 1975 brought with it a relative return to normalcy in the Roloff home. While our home would always be marked by a sort of "crisis management" mentality, it seemed as if the rate and severity of the crises seemed to abate as the year wore on. Sam and I still needed extensive attention, and Josh would still be in a daily battle for survival. And, of course, Ruth was now a teenager, and needed plenty of attention. It was a full plate for our family, but that's the way things had always been for us, and it was almost a relief when we returned to that way of life.

Most families who go through the kind of times we did from January through August of 1975 would feel the need to take a break from things, to just relax for a while and let everything settle. If anyone ever had an excuse to stick with the status quo, if anyone had reason just to kick back and relax—as best they could under the circumstances—it was Mom and Dad. But they didn't. They couldn't. They saw a human need, and they felt compelled to meet that need.

In July of that year—not long after another of Joshua's heart surgeries—

we brought into our San Bruno, California, home a family of eight Vietnamese refugees who had fled their homeland for the United States after the fall of South Vietnam to communism in 1975 following the Vietnam War.

Mom and Dad had a rationale for taking this family into our home, and it was that although they had suffered plenty that year, there were people whose suffering made ours look trivial. Although even they didn't fully understand the extent of the Vietnamese refugees' suffering, Mom and Dad knew they needed to do what they could to help these people who had faced incredible persecution, as well as the deaths of loved ones, just to make it out of their homeland alive.

The eight people—two parents and six children—who stayed with us had fled Vietnam on a small fishing boat with an extended family, making it a total of forty-two people on the boat. They had come from an upper-class background, and several members of the family had worked for the United States or South Vietnamese militaries, making them targets for, at best, "re-education camps," after the war. That meant many if not most of them would not have survived. Their only alternative was to flee the country by boat, facing terrible conditions and the real possibility of dying at sea. They left quickly, taking only the bare essentials with them. When they arrived in the States, they had nothing.

It was quite an experience for my family to have these people from a totally different culture in our home for the better part of a year. Both families adjusted to one another quickly, though. For example, our visitors adjusted to our American custom of all the family members dining together at dinnertime. In Vietnam, children are fed first, then the adults eat. It must have been quite a sight to see fourteen people sitting at the dinner table in the evening. We learned about their culture, too. My mother still knows how to cook great Vietnamese cuisine.

My parents are grateful they had the opportunity to help out that Vietnamese family. They still hear from the family. The kids have gone on to be quite successful in their chosen professions. Seeing these wonderful people succeed in life here has been reward enough for my parents for going the extra mile and taking on an additional responsibility when they had every reason not to.

THE VALUE OF REACHING BEYOND

Reaching beyond the minimum and doing something extra is the way I was brought up, and it's how I live now. I believe that is where life's real rewards can be found. In short, if you put the minimum into life, the minimum is what you'll get in return. I've found this to be true in how I work, in how I operate as a husband and father, in how I run the farm, and in how I relate to people.

I've not perfected the life I'm talking about. But I've been working on it long enough to know it is something that can be done—if a person is willing to apply some of those truths of life I've been taught.

BEATING TALL ODDS

I know you have something going against you that you could use as an excuse for not doing your best. Everyone does. I want to close this book by talking about the things that have helped me overcome my obstacles and enjoy life more than most people would have believed possible.

A GOOD SELF-IMAGE

My physical shortcomings, combined with the way I was raised, have made me very good at making positives out of things that might appear on their surface to be negatives. I'm not talking about just putting a positive spin on a bad situation; I'm talking about actually taking a bad situation and *making* something good out of it.

Much of that ability springs from the fact that I have what I consider a healthy self-image. I've accepted the way I've been made, and because of that, I have been able to use the skills and talents God has given me to thrive in a world that has the potential to present seemingly insurmountable obstacles for me.

I've known people whose physical problems make mine look minor—people horribly burned or disfigured by accidents or birth defects, people confined to wheelchairs for life, people who couldn't move their arms or legs—but who had wonderful self-images. They only had to open their mouths and talk to make people understand that, despite their problems, they felt good about themselves.

I have seen the devastating effects a negative self-image can have on people. I've known little people who are so down on themselves they have a difficult time functioning even minimally in the world around them. I've known too many of them who sink into feelings of hopelessness and disconnectedness from a world that sees them as some kind of freaks.

I know what it's like to be the object of the stares—or to have people look away when I've caught them staring. I understand what it's like to have someone look at me and assume I'm not capable of having a healthy, productive life—a life that includes things like a wife, children, and a career—just because I'm little.

That kind of thing could have shattered me if I'd had a bad self-image or if I'd been self-conscious about the way I look. I was fortunate in that I had a family who promoted the idea I was a person of worth, no matter what I looked like. My parents taught me I was God's creation, a valuable part of the world God had made and put into motion. They taught me from the time I was small that who I really am has nothing to do with my height or what I look like.

Not all people—whether little or average-sized—have that advantage. Not everyone's family teaches intrinsic value and self-acceptance. Maybe yours didn't. So listen to me right now: You are a person with gifts, talents, and value, simply because of who you are.

When people understand this, they not only begin to see themselves in a more positive light, they are also free to pursue excellence in whatever areas they choose.

BE THE BEST YOU CAN BE

I believe that for every person there is at least one area—be it an area of work, play, or relationships—in which he or she excels. Everybody, even the most severely disabled among us, can be good at something! It may take time to figure out what it is, but as you are searching for your area of excellence, I encourage you to be the best you can be in whatever you are doing right now. If you are a computer programmer, work to be the best programmer there is. If you are a writer, make it your goal to be the best writer around. If your job is to clean toilets, be the best to ever scrub a commode.

While you are being the best you can be in your current station in life, think about something you like to do, something you are passionate about. Lock that down. Then ask yourself—and your friends or family—what skills and talents you have that could lend themselves to the thing you like to do. Then figure out what it takes to become the best you can be in that field.

The first thing I tell people who want to be good at something is that they have to become an expert at it. For example, I am considered an expert in what is called in the computer industry "service software." That includes four categories of software, and I've developed a level of expertise in all four. I'm stronger in some than others, but I know each category well. Since I am an expert in the field, I have excelled in it.

You can't skim the surface in knowing about a field if you want to master it. Learn all there is to know about it. I've known too many people who go through life bouncing from career to career like a flat rock on a calm lake. They never get their feet into anything, never earn expertise at anything, and, like the rock, end up sinking in the end.

Ask yourself what it takes to be an expert in a particular field, then do those things. Ask questions of people who know that field, read books about it, and observe all you can while you work in the field. Above all, be ready to acquire some personal experience in the field you want to know. For example, if you want to be an expert in rebuilding engines, you're going to need to rebuild a few.

As you develop your expertise so you can be the best you can be at something, it's also important that you make yourself valuable to others. No matter where you are, no matter what kind of work you are doing, do the things that increase your worth to others, and the opportunities you are looking for will come naturally. Every day on the job, at home, or in social situations, do what you can to make a mark on someone, to make yourself valuable. Make yourself valuable to your boss, your family, your friends, and at the end of the day, ask yourself how valuable you were.

Being the best you can be at something requires that you learn to respect those in authority over you. I know a lot of very talented, skilled people who struggle in the world of work because they can't get along with their bosses. They grumble and complain and bad-mouth their bosses, then they can't understand why they don't get the promotion they wanted or why they don't get the best job assignments.

I've always understood the idea of respecting my boss and committing myself to doing what is wanted—even if I don't agree. In the corporate world, that's called "disagree and commit," meaning that even if you disagree with a decision, you are committed to honoring it because it's the direction those in authority have chosen to take the company.

Being the best you can be at something requires a lot of hard work, perseverance, and sometimes, humility. But it's one of the keys to living an overcoming life, a life that is both enriching and satisfying.

DARE TO DREAM!

No one has ever accomplished something worthwhile without daring to dream about it first. It's safe to say that any great invention or concept started with someone developing a dream, then acting on it. For example, before the invention of the "horseless carriage" someone had to have dreamt up the idea of a self-powered vehicle that could carry people. Before the invention of television, someone dreamt of the idea of transmitting audio and visual images through the air to a receiver.

Before you can set goals, before you can make plans to implement those goals, you have to be able to dream. I'm not talking about idle daydreams or unattainable fantasies, I'm talking about a plan or a desire for which you have developed real passion. I'm talking about a vivid mental picture of something you want to do in life, something that is both visionary and realistic.

From the time I was a small child, I knew how to dream (that's easy to learn when you are confined to a hospital bed for months on end). I can remember lying in my bed dreaming of a go-cart I wanted to build. I thought about how to design the cart so it could take advantage of what I knew was a plentiful natural resource in San Francisco: wind. I dreamed of how to rig a sail on the cart so it could catch the wind and move the cart faster than the go-carts I'd ridden in before.

I tend to dream out loud and on paper. That's how I did it when I first started thinking about the things I wanted to do with the farm—the restoration of the barn, the movable town, the pirate ship, the tree house. As a kid,

I dreamed of the life Tom Sawyer lived, of the adventures he enjoyed, of the people he met. As an adult, I dreamed of constructing a Tom Sawyer world right there in the middle of my farm, where my children could have their own adventures.

I talked about those things to my friends and coworkers, many of whom listened politely, then walked away rolling their eyes and thinking, *Yeah, right!* But I never let that stop me from dreaming and planning. It didn't bother me that my friends thought of me as an eccentric little guy. I had my dreams, and I was going to do whatever it took to see them become reality.

I spent hours sitting at home with a pencil and pad drawing and redrawing tentative plans. Sometimes when I had spare time, I'd just sit and think about how I wanted to design and build the things I desired on the farm. I dreamed of a place where my kids would have a surplus of things they might need to have fun and to entertain their friends. A place where they could use their imagination and build creativity. As time went on, my dreams came closer and closer to reality.

I like to dare people to dream. I love to challenge them to set their sights above where they are, on things they may have thought about but hadn't considered actually accomplishing, and on things that are a stretch for them, yet achievable.

SET HIGH, ACHIEVABLE GOALS

It's important to dream and plan, but it's equally important to set rational goals. A *dream* is an idea or a vision of something you would like to do "one day when…" A *goal* is the dream combined with a plan. For example, when Americans talked in the fifties and early sixties about the possibility of putting a man on the moon, that was a dream. When President John F. Kennedy said he wanted us to put a man on the moon within the decade for a billion dollars, that was a goal because it had scope, a time line, and a named resource.

I love to set goals for myself. I like to have several goals in mind at a given time—keeping several irons in the fire. I like to set short- and long-term goals, goals that are readily achievable and goals I know will be a stretch for me to achieve. Someone I worked closely with once told me, "Matt, you know how to reach out just far enough and pull it in." That defines one of my philosophies in life. I believe in challenging myself and reaching beyond what I am doing now, in setting goals that are difficult but not impossible to achieve.

Another distinction I draw between dreams and goals is that goals are achievable with the resources you have or will have at hand. I believe in setting goals that stretch me, but I also believe in being practical. One of the biggest mistakes people make when they set goals is to set unrealistic ones. For example, I'd never set a goal to make the roster of a National Basketball Association.

Setting goals should also include steps to achieve them. I'm reminded of something Jon Andreasen, my boss at Altos Computer Systems, used to tell me: "You can't get there from here."

I've always tried to live by the old saying, "*Can't* is a four-letter word." It drives me crazy to hear people say they can't do something, but there is value in what Jon told me because it points out the fact that sometimes you have to take a different route to get where you want to go, or that you may need to take additional steps to get there. Another mistake people make in setting goals is trying to get to point D when they are only at A. The error is that they try to bypass steps B and C, thereby setting themselves up for failure or discouragement.

Sometimes the things I want to accomplish are one-step projects. Others—most things, in fact—are projects that take more than one step. For example, building my portable Old West town took several steps, each of which had to be complete before I could move on to the next. I started out with the idea and a few sketches of what the town would look like. I wanted a big tunnel under the town, so I started from the ground—actually lower than that—and worked my way up. I knew it wouldn't be a good idea to just dig the tunnels. I wanted them to be collapse-proof so the kids could play in them safely. I figured out the best way to do that was to dig out a spot in the earth where the tunnels would be, construct the tunnels, then backfill the hole with dirt.

I started by digging a big hole where I wanted the town to be, then sat back for a winter thinking about my next step. I wasn't worried about what my next step would be; I just wanted to get the hole dug then let the idea for the next step come to me. The hole sat out there for a year before I decided how to do it. I used that year to figure out the drainage for the tunnel. I watched how the rainwater flowed in and out of the hole, and I figured out the best way to get the hole to drain into the pond.

Once the tunnel was in place and the hole was backfilled, I set about designing the movable buildings for the town. That, I soon found out, was a new idea; even Disneyland doesn't have a town that can be rearranged.

TIME IS LIMITED...USE IT WISELY!

I would be hard-pressed to think of a resource I value more than my time. Time is a nonrenewable resource: once you use it, you can't get it back. Every hour I spend working, playing, relaxing, or sleeping—and every hour I waste—is an hour I can never get back to use for anything else. For that reason, I am big on using my time efficiently and wisely.

I believe in relaxing. There is nothing wrong with taking a few hours to watch a ball game on TV—although I prefer to attend a sporting event in person if I can get tickets. I have no problem with taking time to read for pleasure or watch a movie. And I am certainly all for spending time and doing things with my family just to be with them.

I've found that when I use my time efficiently, I have *more* time to do the things I do just because I like to do them. One key, I've learned, is to avoid the really big time waster, television.

If I knew someone who said he didn't have time to get done the things he needed to do or wanted to do, the first thing I'd ask him is how much television he watches every day, then I'd tell him to turn if off and go do something else. Television is the biggest time waster around today, especially for people who spend hours a day watching it. TV is a black hole: it sucks in your time, giving little or nothing in return.

I'm not saying you shouldn't watch television at all; I'm simply talking about moderation. I have some shows I watch pretty regularly myself, including news shows such as *20/20*. I like to stay up on current events, and that is one good use for TV. But even when I watch those shows, I'm usually sitting with a pad and paper, making my list of things to do for the next day, or jotting down an idea or a plan.

The way I limit myself when it comes to television watching started when I was a kid because my mother really limited the amount of TV we could watch. Mom took it a step further when I was ten, unplugging our TV set and storing it away. Mom knew what a potential time waster television could have been for us, and she wanted to keep us from falling into that trap. My mother wanted us out playing or in the house reading or studying, and she knew that TV would have cut into our time to do those things. Even when I was in the hospital, my opportunities for watching television were limited by the hospital rules.

That lack of television really helped fuel my creativity when I was a kid, too. Instead of sitting in front of the television, like so many of my friends did, I was out doing things, building things, and earning money. When I could have been watching TV, I was being industrious, starting businesses and inventing things like my automatic newspaper roller (to make my newspaper delivery job easier) and my can smasher.

I've followed my mother's lead in that area, too, limiting the time my kids can watch television to a few shows and some movies we own. I don't know why they'd want to watch TV that much since they have so much to do and so many friends to do it with on the farm.

In addition to turning off the television, I've learned that making lists of things to do for a given day, week, month, or season can be an invaluable tool to help me use my time more efficiently. I've gotten good at making lists. I take some time early in a day to list the things I'd like to do, then I try to figure out how to do them more efficiently. I try to combine two tasks so I don't end up wasting time on both of them. For example, if my list includes taking my car in to get the oil changed and getting a haircut, I do those two things on the same trip—maybe even at the same time if there is an oil change place near my barbershop.

Time is a vital, limited resource for everybody, and using it properly and efficiently is absolutely necessary if you are working to overcome the obstacles life throws your way.

USE YOUR MIND

It may not sound politically correct for me to say it, but I understood at a young age that my physical condition was going to keep me from doing some things others might have a chance to do. I'm very careful when I talk about that not to use the word *limit* because I don't believe my condition has limited me in any way. Rather, it has steered me in a direction I might not have gone had I been tall. It has forced me to further develop talents I might not have otherwise recognized.

Dad always taught me the mind is like a muscle; it needs exercise to grow and expand. He taught me my mind had incredible potential and could solve almost any problem if I would simply learn how to use it.

I remember one example of that from something my parents read to me when I was a kid. It was the story of a Vietnam prisoner of war by the name of Howard Rutledge. The book was called *In the Presence of Mine Enemies: 1965–1973; A Prisoner of War*.

Rutledge would lie in his cell at night and visualize the dream house he wanted to build when he got home. In an effort to fight the boredom, isolation, and suffering he endured in his dark cell, Rutledge visualized every step of the process to build his home, from the basic floor plan to the last coat of paint on the interior. He imagined himself putting the house together board by board, nail by nail, and shingle by shingle. He thought about all the angles, how he would toe-nail each stud, and how he would configure each room. By the time he got out of the POW camp, he had memorized the whole process of building his home. It wasn't long after he got back to the States that he built the house from the plans he had stored—in his mind.

I identified with Howard Rutledge when I was "imprisoned" in the hospitals. I knew what it was like to live in isolation and confinement. Like Rutledge, I learned to use my mind, and it was a skill that would be invaluable to me as I got on with a life that required me to overcome some big obstacles.

PEOPLE ARE IMPORTANT!

No one—from the most severely disabled person to the most completely "whole" in mind and body—will ever accomplish anything great in life unless he or she understands the value of people, the intrinsic worth of every human being just because he or she is a person made in God's image.

I am blessed to have come from a family that taught me to be a lover of people and to respect and appreciate each person I meet, from the "important" to the "least" among us. That is the one way I am most like my father. Dad is a people lover extraordinaire. He's the kind of man who will strike up conversation in just about any social setting, the kind of man who genuinely loves—and *likes*—people just because they are people.

I love interaction with people. Put me in a party, on a plane or bus, on an elevator, in a business meeting, and I'm doing all I can to start a conversation with anyone who cares to talk—and with some of those who don't. My personality is such that I take it as a personal *challenge* when I'm on a plane and the person next to me seems intent on burying his nose in a newspaper or magazine. I like to make a good first impression on everyone I meet. I love to make connections with people, and not just on a one-time basis. I like to give myself and the people I meet a reason to get in touch again. I give out thousands of business cards every year, and I have collected several hundred from people I've met.

I have learned there can be great personal benefit in meeting people and interacting with them. I've learned that a person always has something to offer me and I have something to offer him or her. It may be nothing more than an idea or thought, or it might be something like a major business contact.

I would encourage you to make it a habit to take the time to talk with people you encounter, to make yourself available for conversation, no matter what the setting. Build relationships with people you encounter every day. It's a fun, enriching way to live, but it could also be that the person next to you on the bus or plane or in line at the movie theater could be someone who makes a big difference in some important area of your life.

When you build those relationships, make personal integrity a priority. Treat people the way you want to be treated, and always make sure you keep your word. Make sure you let those people know they are important to you, that their ideas and dreams are important. Be willing to listen to them and be flexible when it comes to considering their ideas. When it's due, give them credit or compliment them on something they are doing well, either for you or for themselves.

When you have conflicts in your personal relationships—and conflicts will come when humans are involved—learn to respond to the situation and not react to it. By that I mean, think through what your words or actions will be when the conflicts arise. Pick your battles, and learn to let it go when someone does something small that offends you or causes you an inconvenience, realizing it could be you who messes up tomorrow.

When it comes to getting angry, if you can help it, don't. I was something of a hothead when I was young. I'd get angry over small things and burn up a lot of emotional time and energy—both of which could've been used for other things. There are times when anger is justified, even necessary. But I've learned those times are fewer and farther between than I thought when I was younger.

Always be gracious to people you meet. My folks, especially Mom, were big on teaching me to be gracious. They both taught us to be independent and not to expect special treatment, but they also taught us to respond graciously to people, particularly when someone offered to help us out, even if we didn't feel like we needed it.

PRAY FOR SOLOMON-LIKE WISDOM

If I had to choose between wisdom and great education, intelligence, or talent, I'd take wisdom every time. I'm a big proponent of formal education—K through twelve, as well as college—and I am certainly glad there are intelligent and talented people in the world. But I don't believe those things amount to much if there isn't a little bit of wisdom thrown into the mixture.

The Bible says King Solomon prayed for wisdom rather than riches, and God honored that prayer by giving Solomon "wisdom and very great insight, and a breadth of understanding as measureless as the sand on the seashore" (1 Kings 4:29). The Bible speaks repeatedly about how we are to pursue wisdom and how God desires to grant wisdom to those who seek it.

Wisdom, to me, is the ability to appropriately and effectively and in a godly manner respond to life's situations by making the right choices. Talent and education might get you to the top in your chosen profession, but wisdom will remind you to stay humble once you get there. Intelligence and know-how will help you achieve and get ahead of the pack in the world of work, but wisdom will help you treat well the people you pass along the way. Hard work will help you take care of meeting your family's physical needs, but wisdom will help you take care of the intangibles of being a spouse and parent.

I've known a lot of brilliant, talented people—people with outstanding intelligence, seemingly unlimited ability, impeccable credentials, and a ton of formal education—who don't have wisdom or common sense, and it limits them. On the other hand, I've met people who have only average intelligence but who know what it takes to successfully handle life's trials and tests.

I've not made a secret in this book of my respect and admiration for my father. I admire and am grateful for how hard he worked to get me through a vital time in my life. I am still amazed at his love for his wife and children, and I think that love has been a cornerstone in my own life. As much as I admire and respect him for those things, I am astounded at my father's wisdom. While my father is of considerable intelligence, he is not a formally educated man. He has the kind of wisdom he has needed to get us through some very difficult times.

As a child, I sometimes prayed for God to make me tall. But there was something in the back of my mind that told me that there was a good chance—a probability—that it wasn't in his will for me to be tall. So I started praying for something I knew God wanted me to have, something I would sorely need in order to make it as a little person in a tall person's world. I may not have called it wisdom at the time, but I knew what I was asking for, and I knew he would give it to me.

I've been blessed with the ability to thrive in a world where a lot of people expected me to merely survive. I've enjoyed things in life that even my own parents wondered if I could ever enjoy. I haven't done it on my own, though. I've done it with the help of a family that has loved me and nurtured me and disciplined me when I needed it. I've done it with the help of friends who've believed in me and looked past my physical appearance to see a little guy with big dreams and ideas.

THE PLACE OF GOD IN MY LIFE

As for me and my household, we will serve the Lord.

JOSHUA 24:15B

I can't remember a time in my life when I thought of myself as an "accident" or as some kind of genetic fluke. Outside of a few short times when I was a kid, I never even wanted to be tall. I've never thought God goofed on me, or that something my mother or father did caused me to turn out the way I did.

I've always felt secure in the fact that I was made the way I was for a purpose. God knew the best way to make me the man he wanted me to be was to make me little. It was his intention for me, not an oversight. That sense of purpose helped give me an attitude of contentment and gratefulness when it comes to my physical stature and disabilities.

People who know me know I'm by no means perfect. I don't think of myself as the stereotypical "man of God." I've had my share of ups and downs in my Christian life. I have struggled with many of the same things most people struggle with, and some things most men don't. I struggle with attitudes and behaviors I know are not pleasing to God.

Do I love God? Yes! Do I believe the Bible? Without a doubt! Do I believe all things work together for good to those who love him? Absolutely. But, despite all that, do I still sin a lot? Yes! I sin so much I sometimes feel guilty just asking for God's forgiveness. But I know from reading my Bible that God's capacity to forgive far surpasses my ability to blow it. I've learned God can use my imperfections—even though it is certainly not his will for me to sin—to keep me humble and to remind me how much I need him. I'm absolutely secure in the knowledge that God loves me and is committed to making me more like Jesus.

I know God is faithful and never changes. Even in some of the lowest times in my life, I've held on to the faith that I am not alone and that God would get me through. Even through the messes I made myself.

ATTITUDE IS EVERYTHING!

Life hasn't always been easy for me, but it's been great because I've had a positive, healthy attitude about who I am. I believe attitude goes a long way in getting you through the obstacles life is sure to put in your way. Attitude is something that comes from deep within you. It is shown in how you respond to the things that happen to you and people who come into your life. It defines who you are as a person.

But how do you go about developing the right attitude? I believe attitude is a manifestation of a person's level of comfort with God's plan in his or her life. There are three steps to that. First, there is the recognition that God, in fact, has a plan for your life. Second, there is the acceptance of that plan. Third, there is the excitement and sense of adventure about the plan.

It cracks me up every time I remember God has already figured out the plan for my life. So really, I can look at the future and say, "No worries." I used to be afraid God wanted me to be a missionary in Africa. I wondered if I could handle it. But now I know I could if that were God's plan for me. More than that, if it were God's plan, I know it would be fun. God wants us not only to accept his plan but to be jubilant about it.

I grew up hearing how I was put on this earth to glorify God and serve him. My father used to tell us something that stuck with me, and we knew to expect to hear it when our family was going through a tough time. Dad would smile (even though he was hurting because of something difficult that was going on), raise his finger, and say, "This is another opportunity to serve the Lord."

Those words seemed to be a reminder to Dad to maintain a positive attitude when everything around him told him to complain. They seemed to help, too, because my father is one of the most positive people I've ever known. To Dad, those words became a replacement for words another man might have said during trying times. Even in the most uncomfortable moments—for example, if he hit his thumb with a hammer—he'd grit his teeth, smile the best he could, raise his finger, and thank God for another opportunity to serve him.

I'M HERE FOR A REASON

I see Jesus Christ this way: God knew his own character is so difficult to understand that he decided he needed somebody human so we could understand what God is like. Somebody to touch and see and hear. That's Jesus. He came to earth and roamed around on the planet for a few years. He put "God things" in terms we could understand because he was human, but he was all God, too. This same God made me what I am. It's my job as a Christian to try to serve him however I can.

In the recent Hollywood film *Simon Birch,* Simon, an eleven-year-old dwarf who has been rejected by his parents, goes on a quest to find God's purpose for his life. He continuously—with great conviction and a wondrous, childlike faith—tells the people he meets, "God has me here for a reason." He says he is "God's instrument." In the end, Simon discovers God's purpose for his life (I wouldn't dream of giving it away). Because of his belief that God had made him for a specific reason, Simon Birch was able to accept himself when others rejected him. He liked who God made him to be.

As I sat in the movie theater watching *Simon Birch,* I felt a strong sense of identification with Simon. We were both little people who believed in a God who had a purpose for our lives. Like me, Simon was a boy who seemingly had a lot going against him, yet he maintained a good attitude about himself and his place in life. That good attitude sprang from his assurance that God didn't make him the way he was or allow him to undergo hardship for no reason.

While most people don't acknowledge it or seek it out—some even spend a lifetime running from it—God has a plan for each person he creates.

Like Simon Birch, we won't always know what that plan is. We may not totally understand why he allows us to live in difficult circumstances. But that life, as difficult as it may be, can be exciting and fulfilling if you can believe that nothing happens accidentally, that God can use any circumstance that is before you, even the most terrible thing you can imagine happening to you.

Once you realize God has a plan for you and a reason for making you the way you are—even if you don't specifically know why he did—you can learn to accept the things that come your way, even the toughest, most trying events you can imagine. Not only can you accept those things, you can actually feel excited about them and give God credit for them.

NOT MY WILL, BUT YOURS BE DONE....

By and large, I've been content being little. I'm being very honest when I say that if someone were to approach me with a new medical procedure or a drug that would make me average-sized, I wouldn't do it. I like who I am and what I am.

However, I do remember as a kid lying in bed praying that I would grow tall and my disabilities would go away. I got tired of being so much smaller than my friends and classmates, tired of not being able to play sports with them without their making allowances for me, tired of being so "different" from everyone else. So I prayed that God would change my body.

Once, when we were living in Pengrove, California, I went with my family to a special church service. It was a good-sized church where some great things were happening. That night, the service was really hopping. They were holding a healing service, and people were walking up to the altar to have the pastor and the elders lay hands on them and pray. I sat there watching this, and I turned to Mom and said, "I want to go up." I truly believed that if I went forward and had them pray for me and believed that God would heal me, I would be healed.

Mom was concerned that I might be bitterly disappointed, that my faith might be shattered if I were to pray for this kind of miracle, only to wake up the next morning in the same condition. As concerned as she was, she also didn't want to stand in the way of this demonstration of faith by her fourth-grade son. As I walked toward the front of the church, Mom prayed for me, asking God to guard my heart against a loss of faith. I asked the pastor to pray for me that night, and he laid his hands on me and prayed that God would bring healing. I never doubted for a moment that a miracle was possible.

But my miracle didn't come that night, not the one I prayed for, anyway.

It turns out that both the pastor's and my mother's prayers were answered that night. I didn't grow miraculously taller overnight. I knew the second I woke up that I was still little and that the condition of my arms, legs, hips, shoulders, and spine hadn't changed. I went to school that day the same way I'd gone the previous week: small and with crutches in hand. Still, I knew something was different. That day, I could just sense my prayers had been answered. I had a great day at school, and I couldn't wait to tell Mom about it.

"You know what?" I excitedly told my mother when I got home. "I think my prayers were answered."

Mom could see for herself that I wasn't any taller, but she could see in my eyes that I believed something wonderful had happened to me. "Really?" she said. "What makes you say that?"

I told her some kids who hadn't played with me at recess before decided to let me play ball with them. I don't know why, but that day they came over to me and said, "Could we figure out how you could play with us? Maybe you get a special rule or something." We made up the rule and I played ball with them. That was it: no miraculous physical healing, no instant height, no new ability to run with the other kids. All I got that day was a feeling of being included out on the playground, something anybody knows is huge in the life of a fourth grader.

What happened that day was certainly a miracle. I had prayed that God would heal me, and although my body was still the same, something inside me had changed. So often, that's the way God works with me. He doesn't change the situation, he changes me.

PRAYER CHANGES THINGS.... OR DOES IT?

My mother doesn't like the saying, "Prayer changes things," because it isn't necessarily true. By that she means that while God can change any circumstance in answer to prayer, he doesn't always do so. When he chooses not to change things, there is a reason for it, a reason we may not, in our limited human reasoning, understand. The great thing about suffering is that it produces people of stronger character and faith.

My mother knows about these things, too, because she learned them firsthand. With three severely disabled boys to raise, my mother spent hours each week on her knees in prayer. There's no doubt she often prayed variations of Jesus' prayer in the Garden of Gethsemane: "My Father, if it is possible, do not give me this cup of suffering. But do what you want, not what I want" (Matthew 26:39b, NCV).

WHOSE FAULT IS THIS?

When we were young, Mom struggled with thoughts of why she and Dad had become the parents of handicapped children. She wondered if she had done something wrong in her life to deserve what had happened, like maybe there was some sin that had brought all this on. She truly believed she was being judged by God, and she carried around false guilt.

Mom was familiar with the first half of the passage in John chapter 9, where Jesus' disciples, who had just seen a man who had been blind since birth, asked Jesus, "Rabbi, who sinned, this man or his parents, that he would be born blind?" Mom had heard and read that verse countless times, but she was afraid to read on. She didn't want to know the answer. She was so filled with guilt and fear that something worse was going to happen to her.

But one day she finally read the next verse. And when she found the truth, it set her free. "'It was not because of his sins or his parents' sins,' Jesus answered. 'He was born blind so the power of God could be seen in him'" (John 9:3, NLT).

Mom realized that having two severely disabled sons—Sam was yet to come—wasn't punishment from God, but a means by which God could show his works in and through us and our parents. She knew then that being the mother of disabled kids wasn't a punishment, but a calling to a ministry and an opportunity to serve God in ways God would equip her for.

Mom realized God had his reasons for allowing me, and later my brother Sam, to be little people, and my brother Joshua to be born with a severe heart and lung defect. It wasn't because anyone had sinned, it was because God had special plans for our family, some of which have yet to be revealed to us.

LITTLE FOR A REASON

Bad things happen to good people. Good people are the victims of tragic accidents and illnesses. Good people endure heartbreak from broken or damaged relationships. Good people lose loved ones to senseless and random acts of violence. In my limited understanding, I sometimes wonder why those things happen.

But I know something good can come out of these situations. When a person knows God and the way he works, things that on the surface appear to be negatives—even tragedies—can be turned into positives.

A great real-life example of that is a beautiful, athletic woman named Joni Eareckson Tada. When she was a teenager, Joni was paralyzed from the neck down in a diving accident. She's spent the past thirty years confined to a wheelchair. Despite all that—*because* of all that, really—Joni has gone on to do great things for God as an author, artist, and speaker. She has written several inspirational books, illustrated others, and is the president and founder of JAF (Joni and Friends) Ministries, an organization that ministers to disabled people.

Joni's story is inspirational to me and to millions of others because it is a great example of someone who underwent something terrible—paralysis—but allowed God to make something positive out of it. Joni went through horrible depression and thoughts of suicide after the accident, but the love of God sustained her and brought her to a point of realizing that something good could come out of what many people would consider a hopeless situation. Her books and speeches have touched the hearts of millions around the world, giving them encouragement to rely on God when something doesn't seem just or fair, or when something devastating happens.

My finite human mind can't comprehend the thoughts of God and what he might be planning for me or why he might be planning it. I don't have all the information I need to figure out why things happen the way they do. I don't understand why God allowed me to be born and grow up a little person with severe physical problems. I don't understand why my brother

Joshua was born with what is basically a terminal illness. I don't understand why my parents were charged with raising three disabled sons. But God does! He knows what we can handle, he knows what will make us stronger yet more reliant upon him, and he knows what situations will make us more useful to him in the lives of other people. He knows what he's doing.

Although my prayers to be made taller weren't answered the way I wanted them to be, I never lost my faith in God. If anything, my faith was made stronger just because of the work God did inside me. It may sound backward, but my faith in God was actually made stronger because he told me, in effect, "No, Matt. I'm not going to make you tall because I have plans for you that wouldn't be fulfilled if you were like everyone else. You are little for a reason, and I'm going to show you that reason in my time."

HE'S IN CONTROL!

While I was developing in my mother's womb and my parents had no idea I would be badly handicapped, God was in control. So, too, when I was a little boy enduring dozens of surgeries and countless hours of rehabilitation. When I was in high school trying to show bigger guys I wasn't going to be bullied just because I was small. When I was working my way up in the computer business in Silicon Valley. Even when I was wallowing in my own stupidity when I was using drugs, *God was in control.* And when I met Amy, married her, and when she gave birth to four beautiful children, God was in control.

God was in control then, and he's in control now. That is what makes my life so exciting. Although I'm no more certain about what will happen next in my life than any other man, I almost can't wait for the challenges that lie ahead—simply because I know beyond any doubt that God is in control.

God has blessed me in many ways, both in the eternal sense and in the temporal. I know everything I have in this world—my home, my family, my cars, and everything else—is passing, temporary. The things that will last, though, are the things God does inside me to make me more like his Son, Jesus.

Other parts of God's plan I don't know because he hasn't revealed them to me and they haven't unfolded yet. My human nature makes me want to know what is ahead, but God doesn't always let me know what his plans are. It's as if he's driving this big, beautiful car that is my life, and I'm just along for the ride. Or maybe it's like a covert operation in the military, and God is the commanding officer. I may not know what the CO's ultimate plan is, but I'm committed to obeying when he tells me to head in a certain direction.

WHAT NEXT?

My life is incredible. No joke. I've enjoyed some great relationships with people as well as success in my chosen field of work. I've been blessed with a beautiful, supportive wife and four great children, and a special farm on which to raise my kids.

I have no reason to believe this situation will change in the near future. However, I know I could undergo a Job-like experience, in which I lose everything I have—my home, my job, even my wife and children. I don't like the thought of that happening, but I know that if it did, God would be there for me, sending me in a new direction in my life.

My wife hates it when I talk like that. She wants things to stay the way they are for us and the kids. But I tell her, "Honey, if God wants to take it all away, then he will. Either way, he's in control." While it scares Amy a little bit to hear me say that, I find it almost exciting. I don't want to lose everything I have, but at the same time I feel a strange sense of exhilaration at the thought of God taking us a different direction, knowing that he will guide our steps and care for us every moment.

That way of thinking is why Job's story is such an interesting one to me. An extremely wealthy man, well known in his part of the world, both for his riches and for his faith in God. When he lost everything, his friends wanted to know what he would do. Would he curse God or would he continue to trust?

If I were in a spot like that, there's no doubt I would be devastated. My friends would look at me and wonder what I'd say about my God now. I wonder, would I be like Job and continue to trust in God, even though I might be miserable and wondering why these things had happened to me? Would I still do what my dad does, which is to raise his finger and say, "This is another opportunity to serve the Lord"?

In the midst of all that, though the pain would be excruciating, I believe God would give me the strength I would need to continue to trust him and glorify his name with all I had left. I believe there would be, deep down inside me, a sense of peace, an assurance that God would bring something good out of this horrible situation.

I believe we are in the midst of some very exciting times. This world is moving along at a breakneck pace, and it doesn't look like things will slow down anytime soon. What's next? I don't have all the answers anymore than any other man does. I just know that God is in control, and he promises victory to those who love him.

APPENDIX A
LITTLE PEOPLE OF AMERICA

Little People of America, Inc. (LPA) is a nonprofit organization that provides support and information to people of short stature and their families.

Membership is offered to those people who are usually no taller than four feet ten inches. Their short stature is generally caused by one of the more than two hundred medical conditions known as dwarfism.

Membership is also available to relatives and interested professionals who work with short-statured individuals.

WHERE WE BEGAN

Little People of America was formed in 1957 when well-known actor Billy Barty made a national public appeal for all little people in America to join him for a gathering in Reno, Nevada. Mr. Barty and twenty other little people joined together for a week of sharing and learning that they were not alone in facing the challenges of dwarfism.

Today, Little People of America, the largest organization in the world devoted to people of short stature, has more than five thousand little people as members with almost that many family members also holding membership. LPA assists in the formation of related groups throughout the world.

WHO ARE WE?

Dwarfs or other people of short statue (either proportionate or disproportionate) come from all walks of life and ethnic backgrounds. Most people with dwarfism are born to average-sized parents with no history of dwarfism in the family.

Although some types of dwarfism may have associated medical complications, most short-statured individuals have a normal life span and normal intelligence. In fact, people with dwarfism have achieved the same range of career paths as average-sized persons, including doctors, lawyers, ministers, teachers, welders, and artists.

Our Parents Group provides valuable information and opportunities for families. Children meet short-statured adult role models as well as other children with dwarfism. It is important to know that they are not alone. Parents exchange ideas and learn about health care, adapting the home and school, laws that address their children's needs, and everyday community experiences.

As adolescence can be an especially tough time for young people with dwarfism, LPA offers support and guidance to teens and young adults on many issues. LPA also publishes the *Parents Forum*, a national newsletter for parents of dwarf children.

WHAT LPA OFFERS

A nonprofit, tax-exempt organization, LPA offers many services to its members and the entire short-statured community. Hundreds of dedicated LPA volunteers throughout the U.S. seek to improve the quality of life for short-statured people everywhere.

LPA offers information on employment, education, disability rights, adoption of short-statured children, medical issues, clothing, adaptive devices, and parenting tips. Information is provided through a national newsletter *LPA Today* and through numerous seminars and workshops. LPA also provides opportunities for social interaction and participation in athletic events.

LPA provides educational scholarships, medical-assistance grants, assistance in adoption, and funds for publications and other projects.

GETTING INVOLVED IN LPA

Many opportunities are open to those who would like to get involved through one of fifty local chapters, which meet monthly. Additionally, regional meetings provide opportunities for exchange of information and social interaction. The LPA annual national conference usually attracts more than one thousand persons for a week full of fun, sharing, and learning. This conference includes workshops, parent meetings, singles get-togethers, teen events, children's activities, fashion and talent shows, athletic events, and nightly dancing. Free medical clinic examinations are available by world renowned specialists in dwarfism. Seminars cover disability rights, medical issues, sibling concerns, adaptive living, sexuality, employment, and a variety of other pertinent topics.

For more information concerning LPA or to see how you can get involved, visit the LPA Web site at www.lpaonline.org, or call 1-888-LPA-2001.

APPENDIX B
FREQUENTLY ASKED QUESTIONS ABOUT DWARFISM*

Q: What is the definition of dwarfism?

A: The Little People of America (LPA) defines dwarfism as an adult height of four feet ten inches or shorter, among both men and women, as the result of a medical or genetic condition.

Q: What are the most common types of dwarfism?

A: By far the most frequently diagnosed cause of short stature is achondroplasia, a genetic condition that results in disproportionately short arms and legs. (The term "disproportionate" is meant only as a point of compari-son with people who do not have achondroplasia or any other type of skeletal dysplasia. The arms and legs of a person with achondroplasia are perfectly appropriate for someone with that genetic condition.) The average height of adults with achondroplasia is four feet tall. Other genetic conditions that result in short stature include spondylo-epiphyseal dysplasia (SED), diastrophic dysplasia, pseudoachondroplasia, hypochondroplasia, and osteogenesis imperfecta (OI). As one might expect from their names, pseudoachondroplasia and hypochondroplasia are conditions that are frequently confused with achondroplasia; diastropic dysplasia occasionally is, too. OI is characterized by fragile bones that fracture easily.

In addition, a support group has been launched for people affected by Kniest syndrome, a relatively rare form of dwarfism. For information, contact Cory and Julia Sondrol, 4956 Queen Ave. South, Minneapolis, MN 55410, telephone (612) 922-6184, fax (612) 922-8732, e-mail sondrols@aol.com.

According to information compiled by the Greenberg Center at Johns Hopkins Medical Center and by Lee Kitchens, a past president of LPA, the frequency of occurrence of the most common types of dwarfism is as follows:

1. Achondroplasia (one per 14,000 births).
2. SED (one per 95,000 births).
3. Diastrophic dysplasia (one per 110,000 births).

These conditions are essentially untreatable, although some people with achondroplasia have undergone painful (and controversial) limb-lengthening surgery. LPA's position on limb-lengthening is that it is unnecessary surgery with unknown long-term results, and that it is far more useful to build a dwarf child's self-esteem. (More information below.)

Proportionate dwarfism—that is, a short-stature condition that results in the arms, legs, trunk, and head being the same size in relation to each other as would be expected with an average-sized person—is often the result of a hormonal deficiency, and may be treated medically.

Overall, there are more than one hundred diagnosed types of dwarfism, and some that have never been fully diagnosed. Roughly one in ten thousand births will be affected.

Q: *What is a midget?*

A: In some circles, "midget" is the term used for a proportionate dwarf. However, the term has fallen into disfavor and is considered offensive by most people of short stature. Such terms as "dwarf," "little person," "LP," and "person of short stature" are all acceptable, but most people would rather be referred to by their name than by a label.

Q: *What is the medical prognosis of a person with short stature?*

A: It varies from condition to condition, and with the severity of that condition in each individual. However, it's safe to say that the overwhelming majority of LPs enjoy normal intelligence, normal life spans, and reasonably good health. Orthopedic complications are not unusual in people with disproportionate dwarfism such as achondroplasia and diastrophic dysplasia, and sometimes surgery is required.

Q: Is dwarfism considered a disability?

A: Opinions vary within the dwarf community. Certainly a number of short-statured people could be considered disabled as a result of conditions, mainly orthopedic, related to their type of dwarfism. In addition, access issues and problems exist even for healthy LPs. Consider, for example, the simple fact that most achondroplastic adults cannot reach an automated teller machine. Dwarfism is a recognized condition under the Americans with Disabilities Act. Information on the ADA is also available directly from the U.S. Department of Justice, which administers the law.

Q: Are dwarfs able to participate in athletic activities?

A: Yes, within the limits of their individual medical diagnoses. For instance, swimming and bicycling are often recommended for people with skeletal dysplasias, since those activities do not put any pressure on the spine. Long-distance running or even extensive walking can be harmful because of the constant pounding, although, as a rule, healthy dwarf children without any unusual orthopedic problems should be allowed to engage in normal running around.

The Dwarf Athletic Association of America (DAAA) organizes competitions at the annual convention of the Little People of America. The DAAA can be reached through Janet Brown, 418 Willow Way, Lewisville, TX 75067, telephone (214) 317-8299, e-mail jfbda3@aol.com.

Q: It's been reported that car airbags can be dangerous to people of short stature. Should they be disconnected?

A: Little people who drive or those who have little persons riding in their cars may want to consider taking such a step. You can find out more at the National Highway Transportation Safety Administration's airbag-information site.

Q: *Do LPs find their portrayal in movies such as* Snow White and the Seven Dwarfs *offensive?*

A: No doubt some do. Many dwarfs, however, are proud of the role of dwarfs in history and in legend, going back as far as the art of ancient Egypt and Greece. What's important is that the average-sized majority recognizes that LPs are fully capable people entitled to respect and equality.

Q: *Can average-sized people become the parents of dwarf children?*

A: Yes. In fact, that's by far the most common situation. LPA is deeply concerned that as it becomes increasingly common to diagnose genetic conditions, including dwarfism, *in utero,* prospective parents will find it difficult to obtain the data they need to make an informed decision as to whether to continue with the pregnancy. Genetic testing carries with it frightening implications for a whole range of issues, including a person's right to obtain medical and other forms of insurance. LPA believes strongly that prospective parents who become familiar with the full, productive lives led by little people will not likely choose termination.

Q: *Can short-statured couples become the parents of average-sized children?*

A: Yes. The odds vary with diagnosis, but a person with achondroplasia has one dwarfism gene and one "average-sized" gene at a particular location. If both parents have achondroplasia, there is a 25 percent chance their child will inherit the non-dwarfism gene from each parent and thus be average-sized. There's a 50 percent chance the child will inherit one dwarfism gene and one non-dwarfism gene and thus have achondroplasia, just like her or his parents. And there is a 25 percent chance the child will inherit both dwarfism genes, a condition known as a double-dominant syndrome, and which invariably ends in death at birth or shortly thereafter.

Q: Has the gene for achondroplasia been discovered?

A: The gene for achondroplasia was located and identified for the first time in 1994 by a team of scientists at the University of California in Irvine. The lead scientist, the late John Wasmuth, urged that in-utero screening for achondroplasia be prohibited except to detect double-dominant syndrome among achondroplastic couples.

Q: What is LPA's position on the implications of these discoveries in genetics?

A: The following is LPA's "Position Statement on Genetic Discoveries in Dwarfism":

The short-statured community and society in general have become increasingly aware of eugenics movements (efforts to improve human qualities by selection of certain traits) in medical history in the U.S. and abroad and the traditional desire of parents to create perfect, healthy children. Along with other persons affected by genetic disorders, we are not only concerned as to how our health needs will be met under dramatically changing health care systems, but how the use of genetic technologies will affect our quality of life, medically, as well as socially. What will be the impact of the identification of the genes causing dwarfism, not only on our personal lives and our needs, but on how society views us as individuals?

The gene for achondroplasia, the most common type of dwarfism, was discovered in 1994. Achondroplasia is caused by a gene mutation that is the same in 98 percent of the cases. The mutation, affecting growth, especially in the long bones, occurs early in fetal development in one out of every twenty thousand births. Since the achondroplasia gene discovery, genes for many other forms of dwarfism have been located and identified, including those for spondylo-epiphyseal dysplasia, diastrophic dwarfism and pseudo-achondroplasia. These discoveries occurred much more rapidly than either the members of Little People of America (LPA) or the medical community had anticipated. Suddenly and unexpectedly, LPA was placed right in the middle of the medical, social and ethical debate surrounding the brave new world of genetic technology. At that time, formal discussions and education on genetic issues had not yet begun within LPA. Most of us, like most of society, had limited knowledge about the Human Genome Project and the social and ethical implications associated with the possible applications of genetic technology. On one hand, the breakthrough may be used to help achondroplastic couples to identify a fetus with "double-dominant" or homozygous achondroplasia, a fatal condition that occurs in 25 percent of births to those couples. It is also possible that the tests for genes causing short stature will become part of the increasingly routine and controversial genetic screening given to all expectant mothers.

LPA's discussion of these possibilities brought forth a strong emotional reaction. Some members were excited about the developments that led to the understanding of the cause of their conditions, along with the possibility of not having to endure a pregnancy resulting in the infant's death. Others reacted with fear that the knowledge from genetic tests such as these will be used to terminate affected pregnancies and therefore take the opportunity for life away from children such as ourselves and our children. The common thread throughout the discussions was that we as short-statured individuals are productive members of society who must inform the world that, though we face challenges, most of them are environmental (as with people with other disabilities), and we value the opportunity to contribute a unique perspective to the diversity of our society.

LPA is revitalizing its public education campaign, so that people of all sizes, including potential parents and health care professionals, will be properly informed of the realities of life with short stature. LPA is made up of over five thousand individuals with more than a hundred types of dwarfism, their families, a medical advisory board, and other friends and professionals. We are teachers, artists, lawyers, doctors, accountants, welders, plumbers, engineers and actors. We represent every nationality, ethnic group, religion and sexual orientation. Many of us have secondary disabilities as well. We are single and married, with families with spouses, parents and children who are average size and dwarfed, biological, and adopted. For LPA members there is a common feeling of self-acceptance, pride, community and culture. Since 1957, LPA has provided peer support, social and educational opportunities to thousands of individuals with dwarfism and their families. We have been educating society and the medical community about the truths of life with short stature and working to dispel commonly held myths. With the discovery of various genes and mutations causing dwarfism, our educational and advocacy efforts have become ever more important, in the face of a rapidly changing genetic frontier.

Q: *We're the parents of a newborn child who's been diagnosed with achondroplasia, and our pediatrician doesn't know anything about it. What should we do?*

A: Make sure your pediatrician sees "Health Supervision for Children with Achondroplasia," an article by the Committee on Genetics of the American Academy of Pediatrics, which appeared in the March 1995 issue of the journal *Pediatrics*. It is an excellent overview to the issues involved in treating a child with achondroplasia.

Q: *We've heard that very young achondroplastic children can run into a variety of complications. What should we be looking for?*

A: Essentially there are three complications that are sometimes found in achondroplastic infants and toddlers. In all likelihood your child will not run into any of these problems, but she or he should be evaluated for them nevertheless. They are:

- Compression of the brain stem resulting from the top of the spinal column, known as the foramen magnum, being too small to accommodate the spinal cord. Symptoms include central apnea (a condition that causes a person to stop breathing frequently while sleeping) and a general failure to thrive. This condition is treated through surgery, and children who have undergone this operation tend to do very well.
- Hydrocephalus, the technical term for excess fluid on the brain, resulting from the drainage openings in the skull being of insufficient size. All people with achondroplasia have some hydrocephalus, and no harm generally results. In addition, all people with achondroplasia have slightly enlarged heads, which can sometimes create the appearance of a problem where there is none. Nevertheless, occasionally hydrocephalus can present a problem, in which case a shunt may be surgically implanted to drain excess fluid.
- Obstructive apnea resulting from an infant's or very young child's airways being too small or improperly shaped. The child stops breathing and wakes up frequently during the night (unfortunately, as is generally the case with apnea, these moments of wakefulness are fleeting and often go undetected by parents), sweats, snores, and fails to thrive. Depending on the severity, a physician may recommend waiting until the child outgrows the problem; monitoring the child's oxygen levels and trying treatments such as supplemental oxygen and/or CPAP (or BPAP), a treatment device that provides pressure to the lungs; or, in rare instances, performing a tracheostomy to circumvent the tiny upper airways until those airways have a chance to grow.

All of these problems, as well as others, are discussed in more detail in "Health Supervision for Children with Achondroplasia."

Q: My dwarf child will soon undergo surgery. What special considerations regarding anesthesia should be taken into account?

A: In general, the anesthesiologist needs to be careful not to hyperextend your child's neck as much as she or he might with a non-dwarf child.

Also, dosage should be regulated by your child's weight rather than age.

Please be sure your child's doctors have seen the article "Dwarfs: Pathophysiology and Anesthetic Implications," by Berkowitz, Raja, Bender, and Kopits, in the October 1990 issue of the medical journal *Anesthesiology* (Volume 73, Number 4, pages 739–759).

Q: Can you recommend any books?

A: Yes. Two excellent books by medical anthropologist Joan Ablon, *Little People in America* and *Living with Difference*, discuss the social dimensions of dwarfism, both on LPs and their families. *Dwarfism: The Family & Professional Guide*, by the Short Stature Foundation & Information Center, is a good introductory resource, and it's currently being reworked. *Thinking Big*, by Susan Kuklin, is a portrait/photo essay of an eight-year-old girl with achondroplasia that is an outstanding introduction for a young child with achondroplasia. There are a number of other books that are also helpful. Most of these are listed in LPA's newsletter, *LPA Today*, which members receive as part of their dues.

Q: The children at my child's school don't understand dwarfism, and they taunt and tease her. What should I do?

A: Opinions vary, and there is probably not any one-answer-fits-all solution. For some answers, you might want to buy a slide show that's been transferred to videotape called "What Children Want To Know About Little People." For information on how to order this twenty-dollar tape, contact Lenette Sawisch at 3725 West Holmes Road, Lansing, MI 48911-2106, telephone (517) 393-3116; or send e-mail to sawisch@voyager.net.

Q: Does Little People of America have any special resources for parents?

A: Yes. Contact LPA's national parent coordinators, Rob and Betty Jacobsen, at rbjake@teleport.com.

Q: We don't want our child to be treated differently from other children. We've heard about a miraculous operation to lengthen an achondroplastic dwarf's legs and arms. Should we consider this?

A: As a general statement of philosophy, most members of the dwarf community believe that no child should undergo surgery unless it is for a treatable medical condition that will improve her or his health. Limb-lengthening surgery, by contrast, does not address any medical condition. Instead, it permanently weakens healthy arms and legs simply so the person who is operated on looks more like the average-sized majority.

Moreover, a person who's had her or his limbs lengthened still has achondroplasia. She or he is just as likely to experience orthopedic problems with age, and just as likely to pass on the gene—and now may suffer from long-term side effects of the surgery as well. Dwarfism is a genetic difference, not a disease, and many dwarfs are proud of not being like everyone else. Oftentimes a fourteen-year-old child who, because of teenage insecurity and peer pressure, wants his limbs lengthened will mature into an adult who is proud of who he is.

Limb-lengthening surgery involves cutting leg and arm bones, constructing metal frames around the limbs, and inserting pins into the bones to move the cut ends apart. New bone tissue fills in the gap, thus increasing length. The procedure is extremely painful, and it often lasts several years. The most common complications are:

- Bending or twisting of the bone at the site where it is cut.
- Nerve damage caused by the metal devices that are inserted into the bones. This can result in paralysis of the limb.
- If the length is increased too much, the muscle and skin will be stretched too tightly over the limb. This locks the limb out, either straight or bent, and leaves the person unable to control the limb. The only way to overcome this problem is to go back into surgery and shorten the bone.
- Any time a major bone is broken or cut, there is a risk of releasing fat emboli into the bloodstream, which can cause death.

Q: If limb-lengthening is such a terrible procedure, why would anyone go through it?

A: There are some people who've been quite happy with the results. For instance, we recently heard from a person with achondroplasia who thought LPA's assessment of the surgery was too harsh. He told us that he went through the procedure between 1988 and 1991, increasing his height from 3-11 to 5-1 and having his arms lengthened as well. Although he acknowledged that it was a painful procedure, he hastened to add that it was not unbearable by any means. He also believes his arms and legs are stronger than when he began the procedure, that his back is straighter, and that, overall, he is medically better off today than he was before the surgery. Another person with achondroplasia, Gillian Mueller, has written very eloquently about her positive experience with limb-lengthening surgery.

With all due respect, it seems impossible that his arms and legs are stronger as a result of the surgery. It's possible that they're stronger because of the rehabilitation he underwent. But even advocates of the surgery have acknowledged that there may be long-term weakening of the limbs and an increased risk of arthritis.

There is one known medical benefit to limb-lengthening: the patient's back comes into better alignment, and swayback is reduced, which can result in fewer lower-back problems over the long term.

What follows is the LPA Medical Advisory Board's position paper on this issue:

The techniques for leg lengthening were originally developed for correction of limb length discrepancy and are considered the accepted therapy. Particularly in Europe and Russia, similar surgical techniques have been modified for use in symmetric lengthening in short individuals. Though this new application has generated widespread interest, it has also created controversy among medical professionals, persons of short stature, and their families.

There are no established medical indications for symmetric extended limb lengthening (ELL) at this time. However, it may have benefit in preventing orthopedic and neurological complications of the skeletal dysplasias while the function is primarily being performed for adaptive, cosmetic, and psychosocial reasons.

Nationwide research is being done on the safety and long-term functional outcome of the procedure. Experimental protocols to assess benefits and risks of ELL are being carefully drawn. The Medical Advisory Board would welcome the opportunity to review additional protocols, to assure that projects meet the standards of modern scientific research, and to protect persons from undue risk.

The complications of ELL are numerous. These include:

- Nerve injury
- Vascular injury
- Infections
- Angulations
- Non-union
- Paralysis
- Increased hip flexion leading to dislocation of the hip
- Predisposition to early osteoarthritis
- Reabsorption of the bone ends
- Fractures
- Unequal limb lengths

Although the acute complication rate associated with ELL has been reduced, it is still substantial. Furthermore, the long-term stability of limb lengthening has not been determined, particularly subject to physical (such as pregnancy) and hormonal stress.

At this point we consider the use of ELL to increase stature to be experimental. We caution individuals and their families who choose this procedure to select as the site an institution with a multidisciplinary program with special emphasis and expertise in skeletal dysplasia. The institution should be equipped to follow the patient for a decade or more.

This is what patients should have prior to initiation of ELL:

- Confirmation of short-stature diagnosis. Relative risks and benefits are different for the many types of skeletal dysplasias.
- Counseling concerning the natural history and genetic implications of the relevant skeletal dysplasia, independent of ELL.
- Adequate discussion of benefits and risks (including medical complications, fiscal issues, educational and psychological concerns). It is recommended that prospective patients be of an age to participate fully in the decision-making process.

We recommend that before, during, and after that all subsequent ELL evaluations include:

- Orthopedic assessment
- Physical-therapy assessment, including evaluation of mobility, activity, functional limitations, etc.
- Clinical neurological evaluations
- Electrophysiologic testing, including nerve-conduction velocities, and electromyography—and somatosensory-evoked potentials
- Peripheral vascular assessment
- Psychological evaluation, including self-image, body image, peer relationship, and family relationships

All these evaluations will require cooperative involvement of orthopedists, physical and occupational therapists, medical geneticists, radiologists, neurologists, clinical electrophysiologists, peripheral vascular specialists, psychologists and/or psychiatrists, and social workers in longitudinal management.

As a group, what we are trying to impart is that ELL is a complex procedure with far-reaching implications. Complete success is not guaranteed. We caution prospective patients and their families to seek out only institutions that can offer the broad, multidisciplinary approach that is needed. An institution ill-equipped to handle the multiple demands of this procedure should not even be considered.

We are certainly not trying to discourage anyone of short stature from exploring extended limb lengthening. That is not our purpose. Our purpose is to call for a careful assessment of institution and personnel, as well as all risks and benefits.

Q: *Is it possible to adopt children with dwarfism?*

A: Yes. Children are available both in the United States and abroad. There are no shortcuts, however. Adopting a dwarf child is every bit as challenging and arduous a process as adopting an average-stature child. For more information, please contact Joy Wyler, who runs LPA's adoption program, at jwyler@cmh.edu. For more information, Danny Black maintains an LPA adoption Web site.

*All information printed by permission.